BUILD TOY AIRPLANES

10 FULL-SIZE ALL WOOD TOY AIRPLANE PATTERNS

John W. Lewman
Cynthia A. Lewman

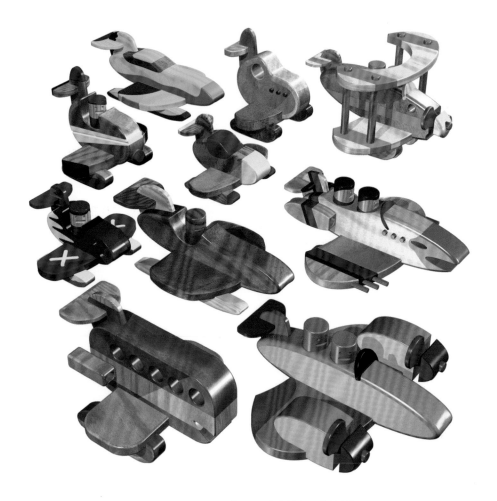

BUILD TOY AIRPLANES
10 FULL-SIZE ALL WOOD
TOY AIRPLANE PATTERNS

Toymaker Press is dedicated to providing you with the information and ideas you need to develop your skills as a toymaker. We welcome your comments and any suggestions about this collection of toy plans.

Email: johnlewman@toymakerpress.com

©2010
John W. Lewman
All rights reserved
Printed in China
First edition

Toymaker Press, Inc.
Shawnee, KS 66216
www.toymakerpress.com

ISBN 978-1-4507-0043-6

90000>

9 781450 700436

Stunt Rider Pg 49

BUILD TOY AIRPLANES

10 FULL-SIZE ALL WOOD
TOY AIRPLANE PATTERNS

Pocket Rocket Pg 7

TABLE OF CONTENTS

Cloud Chaser Pg 11

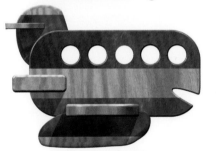

Sky King Pg 37

Figure Eight Pg 25

Zipper Pg 33

Freedom Fighter Pg 43

Private Eye Pg 21

Aero Speeder Pg 15

Sport Twin Pg 55

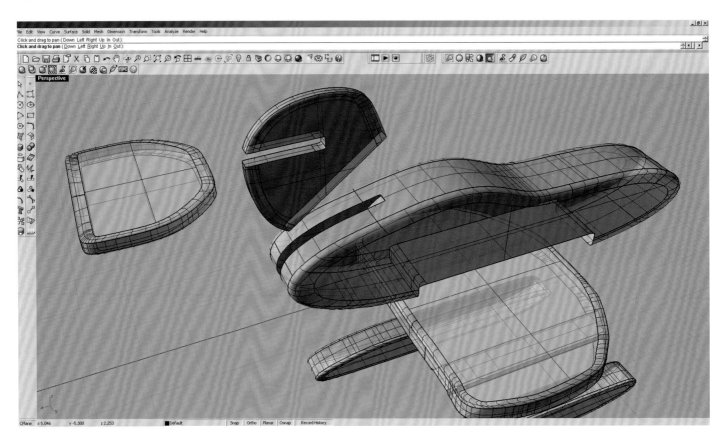

AERO SPEEDER PAGE 15

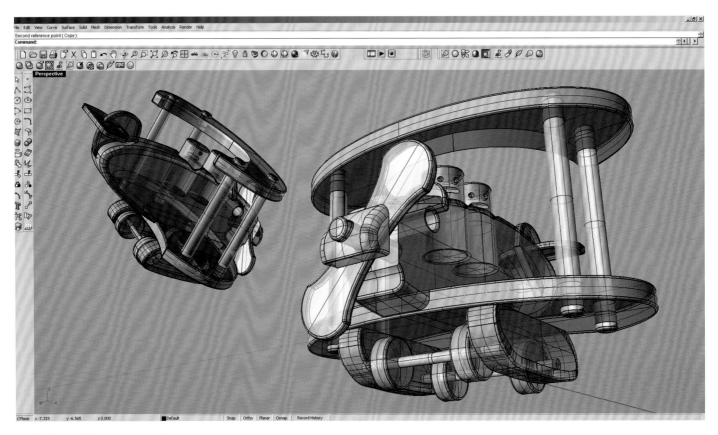

STUNT RIDER PAGE 49

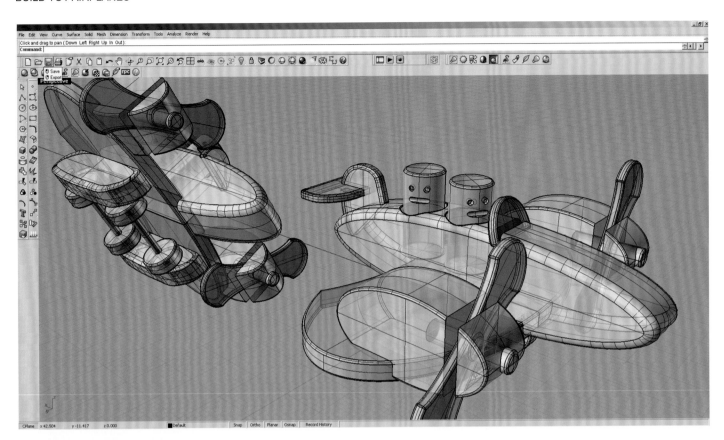

SPORT TWIN PAGE 55

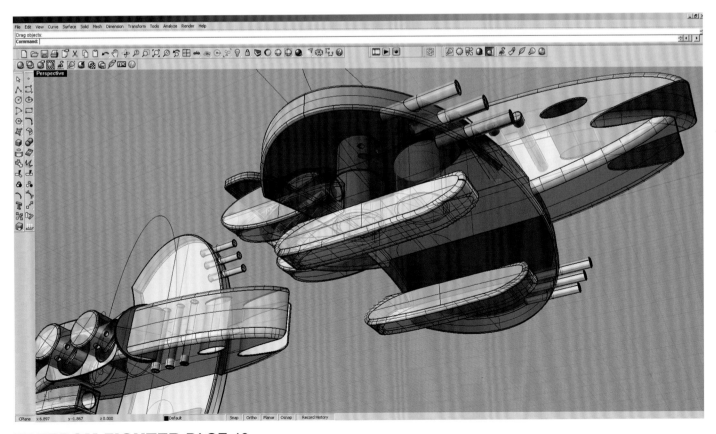

FREEDOM FIGHTER PAGE 43

POCKET ROCKET

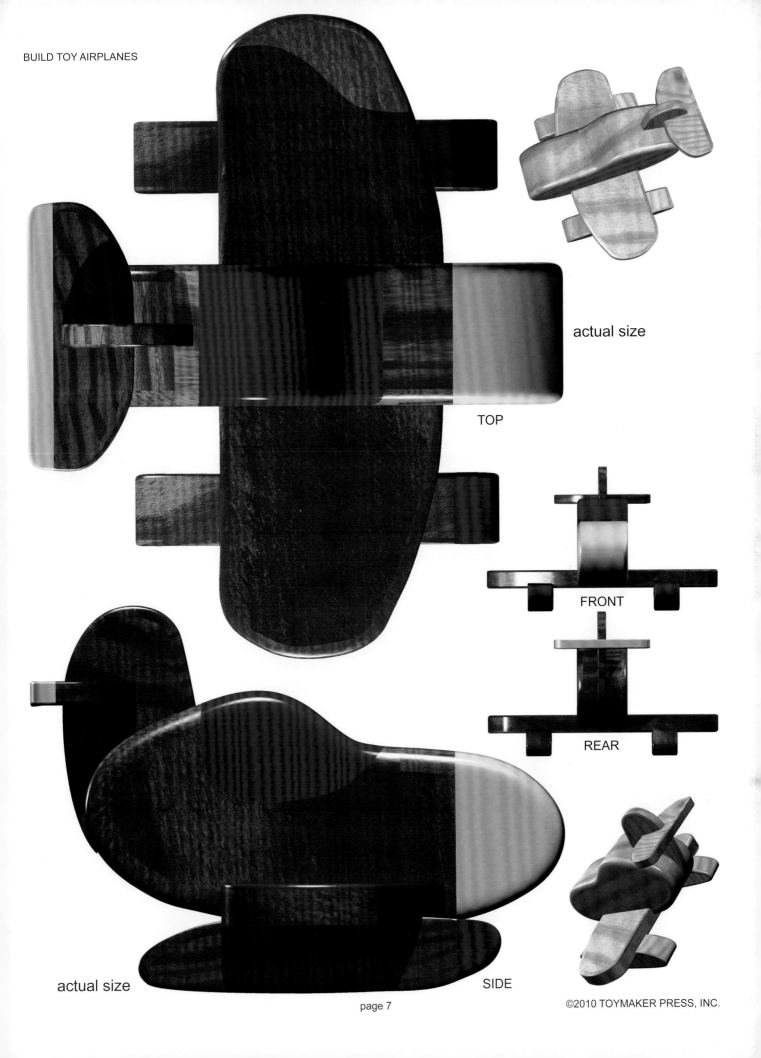

BUILD TOY AIRPLANES

actual size

TOP

FRONT

REAR

actual size

SIDE

BUILD TOY AIRPLANES

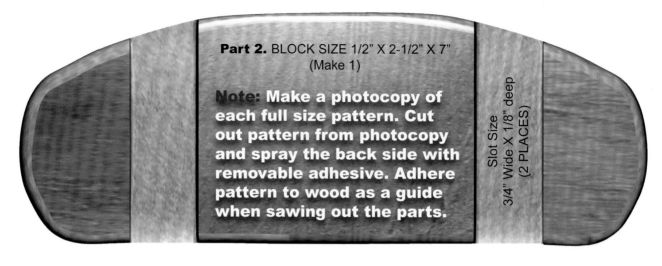

Part 2. BLOCK SIZE 1/2" X 2-1/2" X 7"
(Make 1)

Note: Make a photocopy of each full size pattern. Cut out pattern from photocopy and spray the back side with removable adhesive. Adhere pattern to wood as a guide when sawing out the parts.

Slot Size
3/4" Wide X 1/8" deep
(2 PLACES)

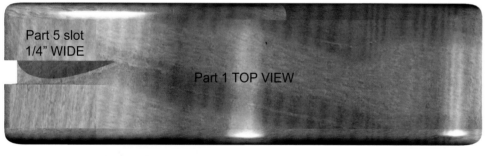

Part 3. BLOCK SIZE 3/4" X 1" X 4-1/4"
(Make 2)

Part 5. BLOCK SIZE
1/4" X 1-5/8" X 3"
(Make 1)

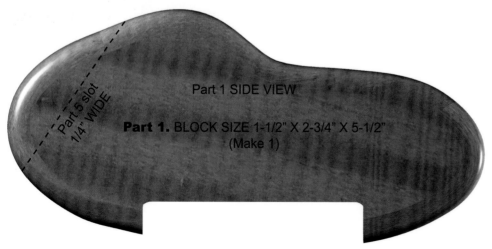

Part 5 slot
1/4" WIDE

Part 1 TOP VIEW

Part 5 slot
1/4" WIDE

Part 1 SIDE VIEW

Part 1. BLOCK SIZE 1-1/2" X 2-3/4" X 5-1/2"
(Make 1)

Part 4. BLOCK SIZE 1/4" X 1-1/4" X 3"
(Make 1)

NOTE: All dimensions are for block size prior to cutting to shape.

NOTE: Add radius to edges with sandpaper or router.

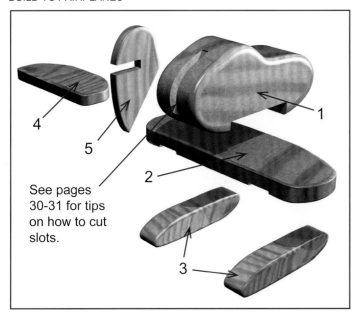

See pages 30-31 for tips on how to cut slots.

1. Add woodworker's white glue to slots in Part 2. Press Part 3 in place in both slots. Let assembly dry before proceeding.

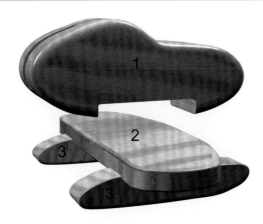

2. Apply woodworker's white glue to large slot in bottom of Part 1. Press Part 1 into position in the middle of Part 2 as shown above. Let dry.

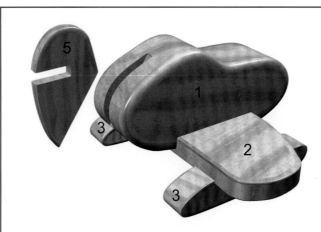

3. Apply woodworker's white glue to slot in top of Part 1. Press Part 5 into position in the slot in middle of Part 1 as shown above. Let dry.

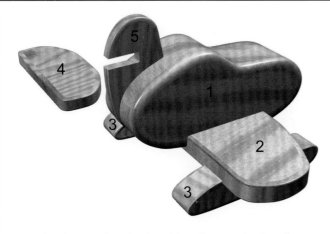

4. Apply woodworker's white glue to slot in edge of Part 5. Press Part 4 into position into Part 5 of the assembly as shown above. Let dry.

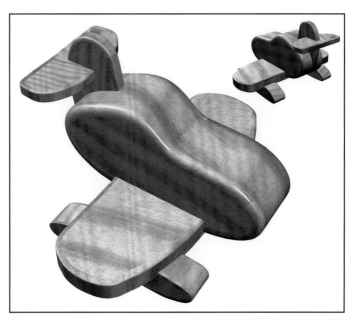

CLOUD CHASER

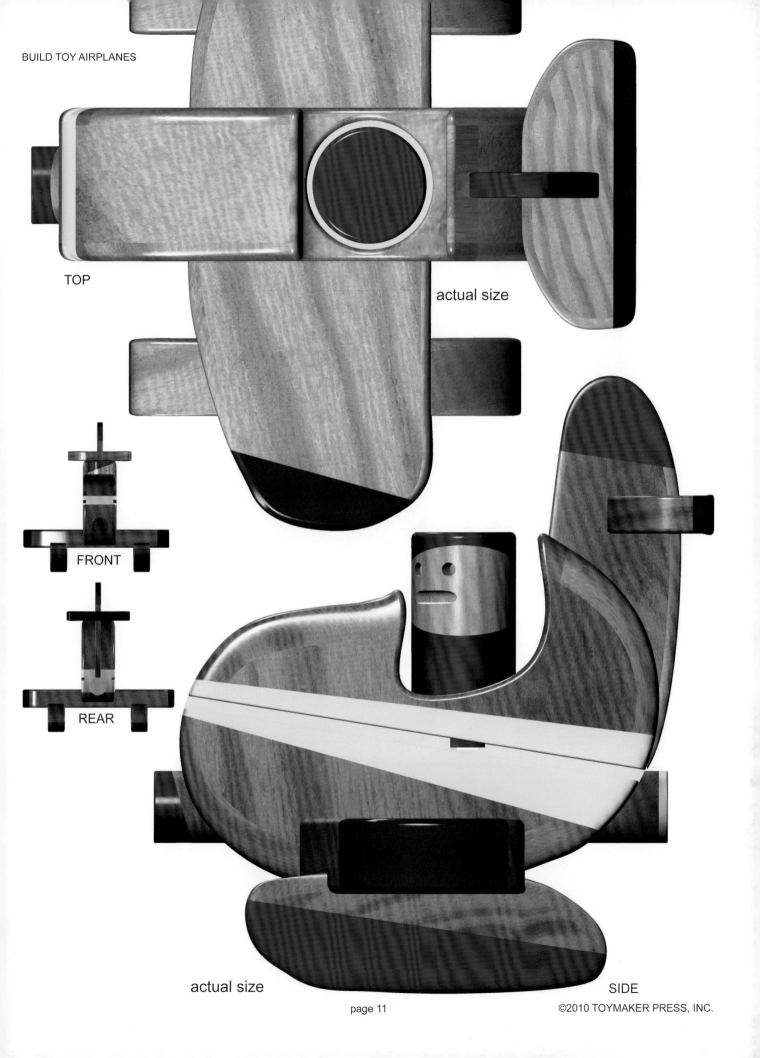

BUILD TOY AIRPLANES

TOP

actual size

FRONT

REAR

actual size

SIDE

BUILD TOY AIRPLANES

Part 5 slot 1/4" WIDE

HOLE
1-1/4" DIA.
1-5/8" DEEP

Part 1 TOP VIEW

Part 6 hole
3/4" DIA. X
1" DEEP
(Make 2)

Part 3. BLOCK SIZE 3/4" X 1-1/2" X 4-1/4" (Make 2)

HOLE
1-1/4" DIA.
1-5/8" DEEP
from top edge

1/8" X 1/8" Decorative slot both sides (not required)

Part 6. DOWEL SIZE 3/4" DIA. X 1-1/2" (Make 2)

Part 5 slot 1/4" WIDE

Part 1. BLOCK SIZE 1-1/2" X 4" X 5-1/2" (Make 1)

Part 1 SIDE VIEW

Part 6 hole
3/4" DIA. X
1" DEEP
(Make 2)

Part 5. BLOCK SIZE 1/4" X 1-5/8" X 4-1/2" (Make 1)

Part 7. DOWEL SIZE 1-1/8" DIA. X 2-1/4" (Make 1)

Part 4. BLOCK SIZE 1/4" X 1-1/4" X 3" (Make 1)

Part 2. BLOCK SIZE 1/2" X 2-1/2" X 7" (Make 1)

Note: Make a photocopy of each full size pattern. Cut out pattern from photocopy and spray the back side with removable adhesive. Adhere pattern to wood as a guide when sawing out the parts.

Slot Size 3/4" Wide X 1/8" deep (2 PLACES)

NOTE: All dimensions are for block size prior to cutting to shape.

BUILD TOY AIRPLANES

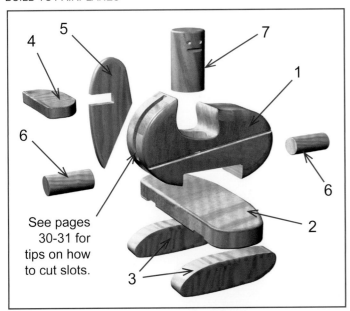

See pages 30-31 for tips on how to cut slots.

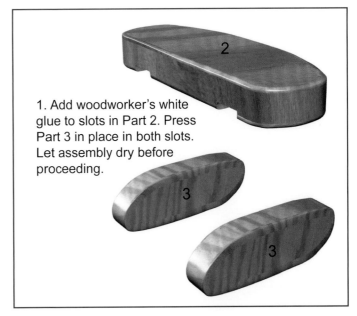

1. Add woodworker's white glue to slots in Part 2. Press Part 3 in place in both slots. Let assembly dry before proceeding.

2. Apply woodworker's white glue to large slot in bottom of Part 1. Press Part 1 into position in the middle of Part 2 shown above. Let dry.

3. Apply woodworker's white glue to front and rear holes in Part 1. Press Part 6 into position in front and rear of Part 1 shown above. Let dry.

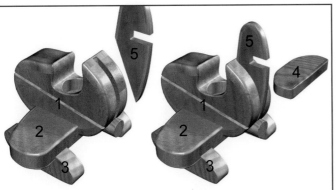

4. Apply woodworker's white glue to rear slot in middle of Part 1. Press Part 5 into position in the middle of Part 1 shown above. Let dry.

5. Apply woodworker's white glue to slot in edge of Part 5. Press Part 4 into the slot in the edge of Part 5 as shown above. Let dry.

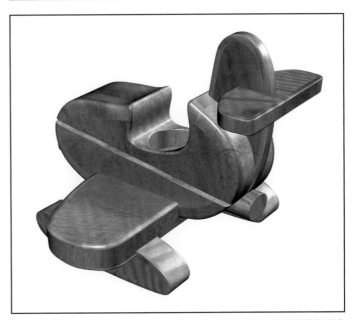

AERO SPEEDER

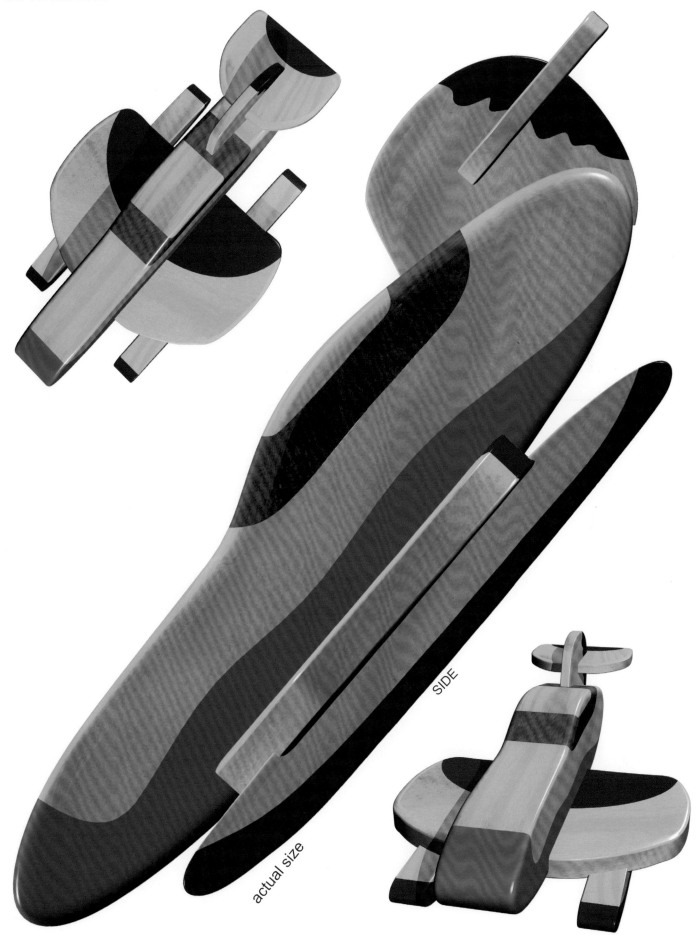

actual size

SIDE

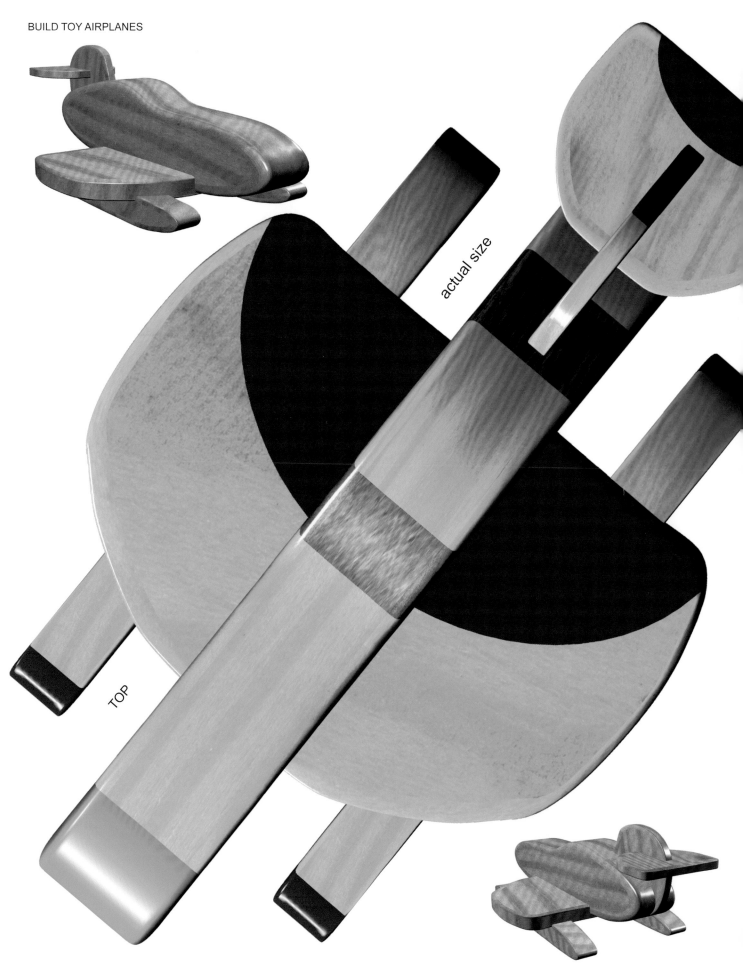

actual size

TOP

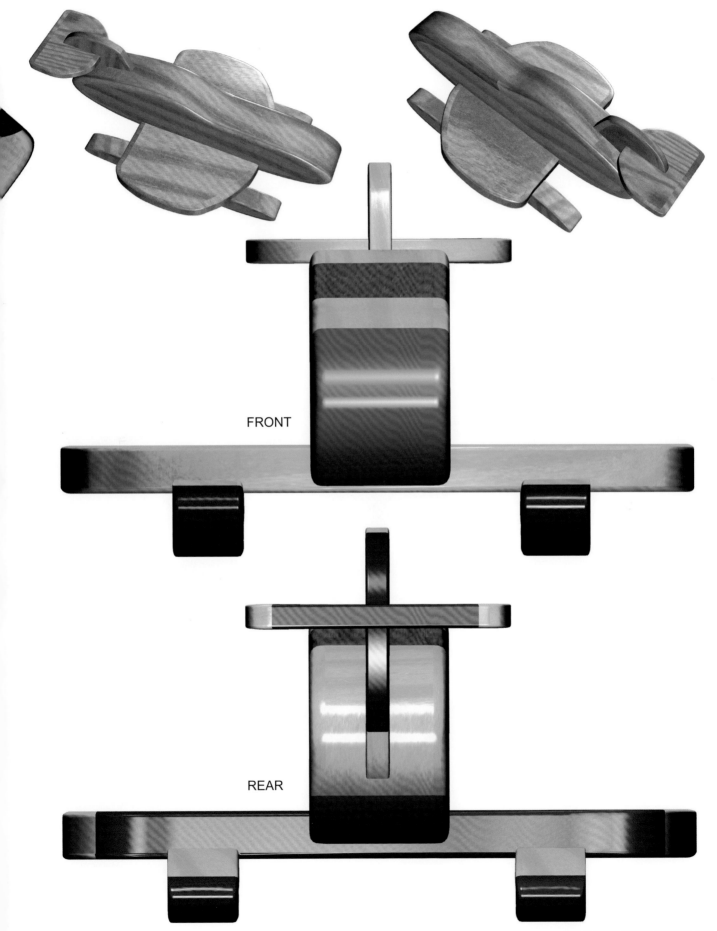

FRONT

REAR

BUILD TOY AIRPLANES

Part 2. BLOCK SIZE 1/2" X 5" X 7-1/2"
(Make 1)

Part 3. BLOCK SIZE 3/4" X 1" X 8"
(Make 2)

Note: Make a photocopy of each full size pattern. Cut out pattern from photocopy and spray the back side with removable adhesive. Adhere pattern to wood as a guide when sawing out the parts.

Slot Size
3/4" Wide X 1/8" deep
(2 PLACES)

Part 1. BLOCK SIZE 1-1/2" X 2-3/4" X 10-1/2"
(Make 1)

Part 5. BLOCK SIZE
1/4" X 2-3/4" X 3-1/4"
(Make 1)

Part 5 slot
1/4" WIDE

Part 4. BLOCK SIZE 1/4" X 3" X 4"
(Make 1)

NOTE: All dimensions are for block size prior to cutting to shape.

NOTE: Add radius to edges with sandpaper or router.

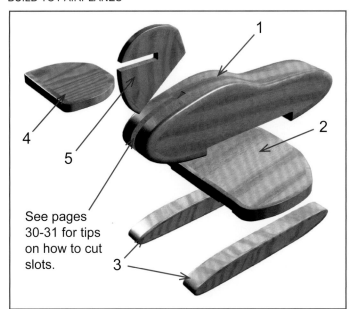

See pages 30-31 for tips on how to cut slots.

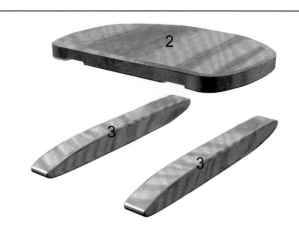

1. Add woodworker's white glue to slots in Part 2. Press Part 3 in place in both slots. Let assembly dry before proceeding.

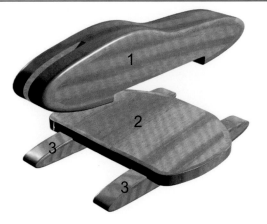

2. Apply woodworker's white glue to large slot in bottom of Part 1. Press Part 1 into position in the middle of Part 2 as shown above. Let dry.

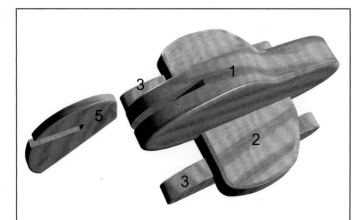

3. Apply woodworker's white glue to slot in top of Part 1. Press Part 5 into position into the slot in middle of Part 1 as shown above. Let dry.

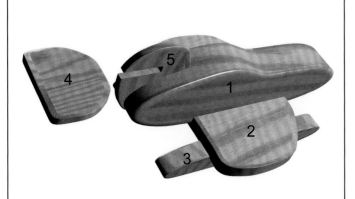

4. Apply woodworker's white glue to slot in edge of Part 5. Press Part 4 into position in the slot in Part 5 as shown above. Let dry.

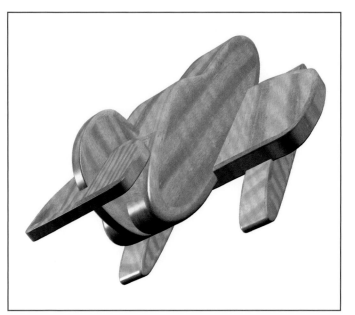

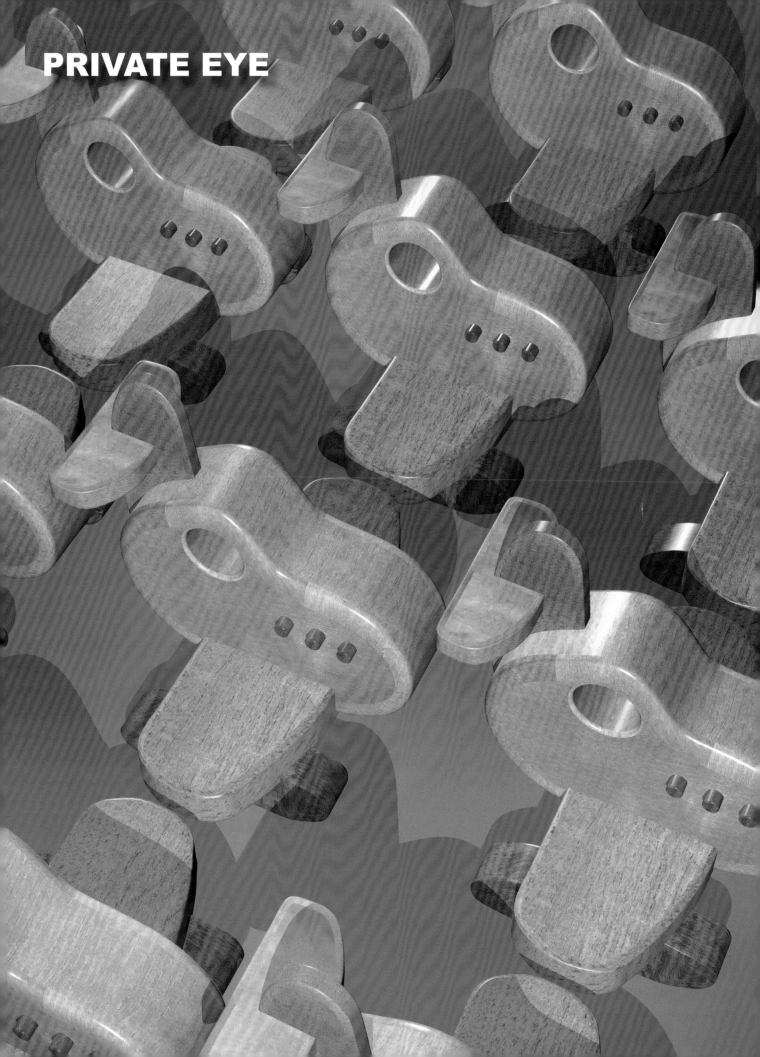

PRIVATE EYE

actual size

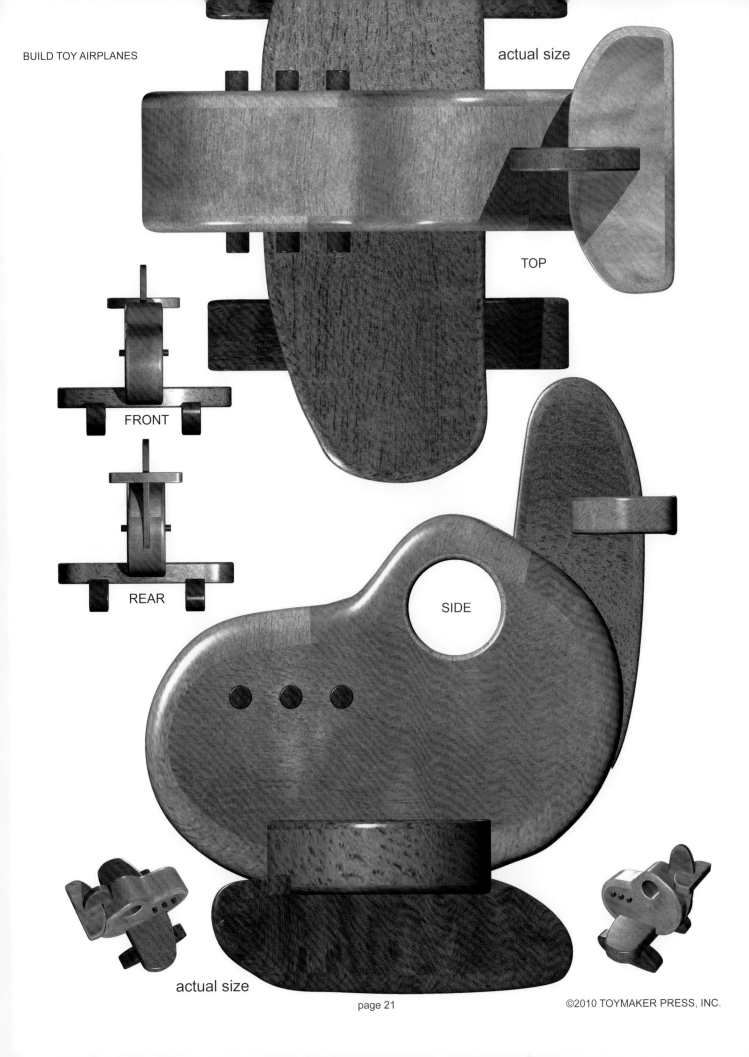

TOP

FRONT

REAR

SIDE

actual size

NOTE: Patterns shown are full size.

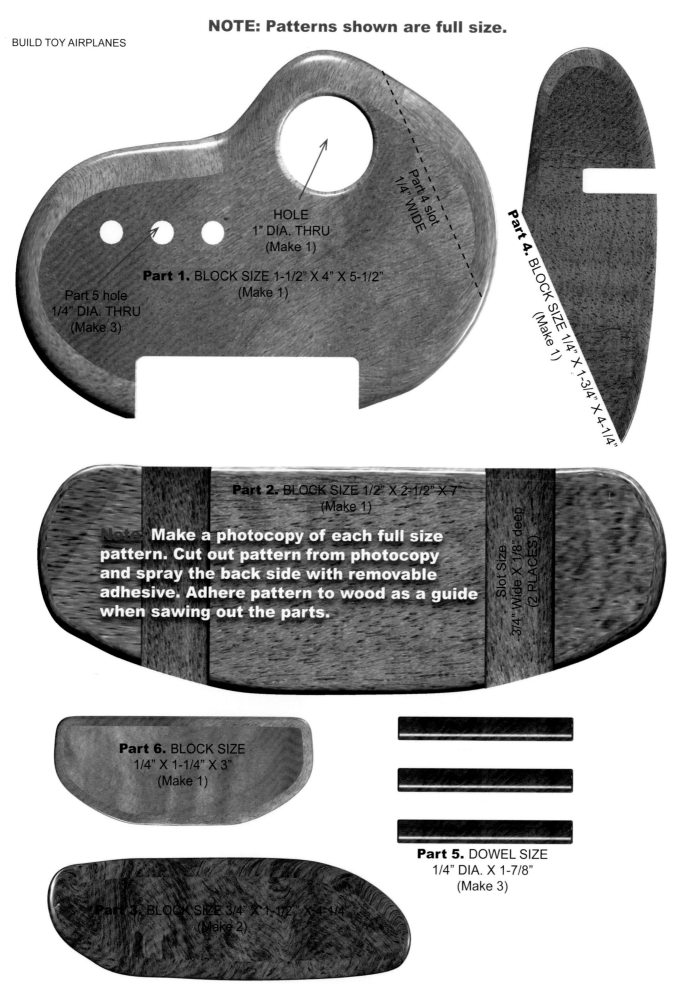

Part 4 slot
1/4" WIDE

HOLE
1" DIA. THRU
(Make 1)

Part 4. BLOCK SIZE 1/4" X 1-3/4" X 4-1/4"
(Make 1)

Part 1. BLOCK SIZE 1-1/2" X 4" X 5-1/2"
(Make 1)

Part 5 hole
1/4" DIA. THRU
(Make 3)

Part 2. BLOCK SIZE 1/2" X 2-1/2" X 7"
(Make 1)

Note: Make a photocopy of each full size pattern. Cut out pattern from photocopy and spray the back side with removable adhesive. Adhere pattern to wood as a guide when sawing out the parts.

Slot Size
3/4" Wide X 1/8" deep
(2 PLACES)

Part 6. BLOCK SIZE
1/4" X 1-1/4" X 3"
(Make 1)

Part 5. DOWEL SIZE
1/4" DIA. X 1-7/8"
(Make 3)

Part 3. BLOCK SIZE 3/4" X 1-1/2" X 4-1/4"
(Make 2)

NOTE: All dimensions are for block size prior to cutting to shape.

BUILD TOY AIRPLANES

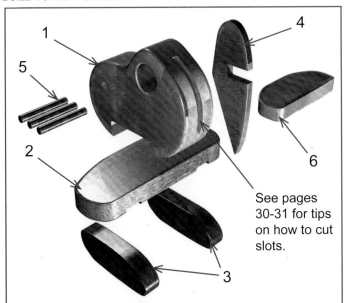

See pages 30-31 for tips on how to cut slots.

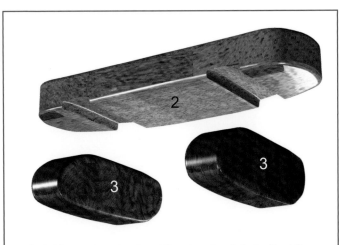

1. Add woodworker's white glue to slots in Part 2. Press Part 3 in place in both slots. Let assembly dry before proceeding.

2. Apply woodworker's white glue to large slot in bottom of Part 1. Press Part 1 into position in the middle of Part 2 as shown above. Let dry.

3. Apply woodworker's white glue to the 3 small holes in side of Part 1. Press Part 5 into position in the 3 holes as shown above. Let dry.

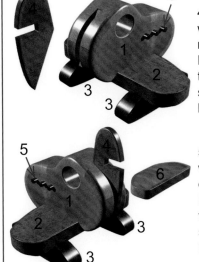

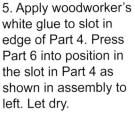

4. Apply woodworker's white glue to slot in middle of Part 1. Press Part 4 into position in the slot in Part 1 as shown in assembly to left. Let dry.

5. Apply woodworker's white glue to slot in edge of Part 4. Press Part 6 into position in the slot in Part 4 as shown in assembly to left. Let dry.

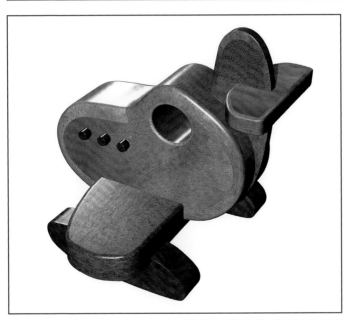

FIGURE EIGHT

SIDE

actual size

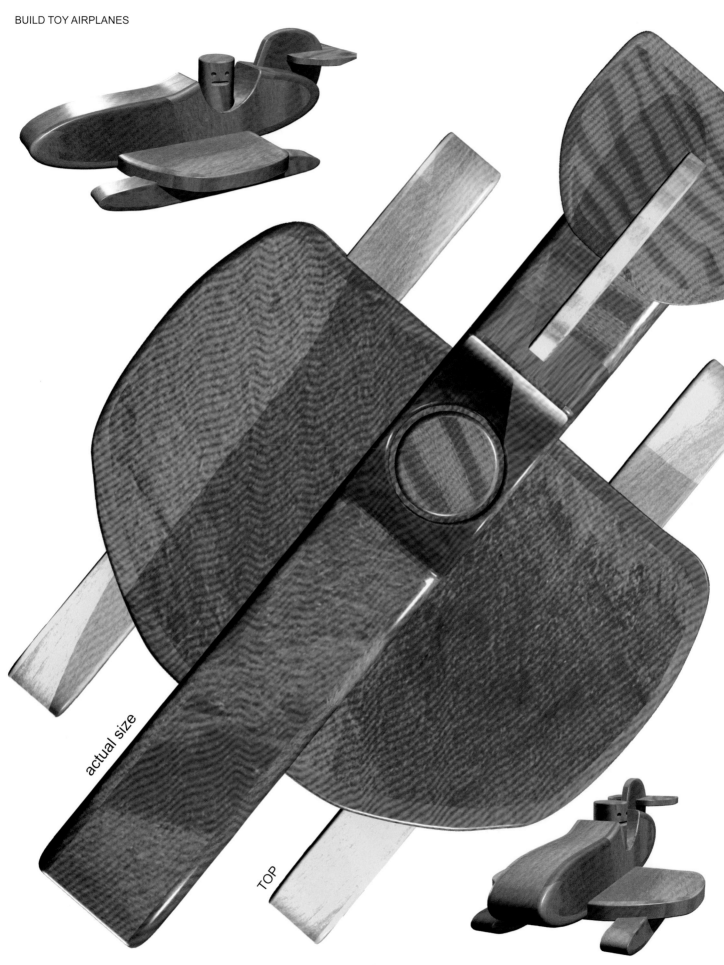

actual size

TOP

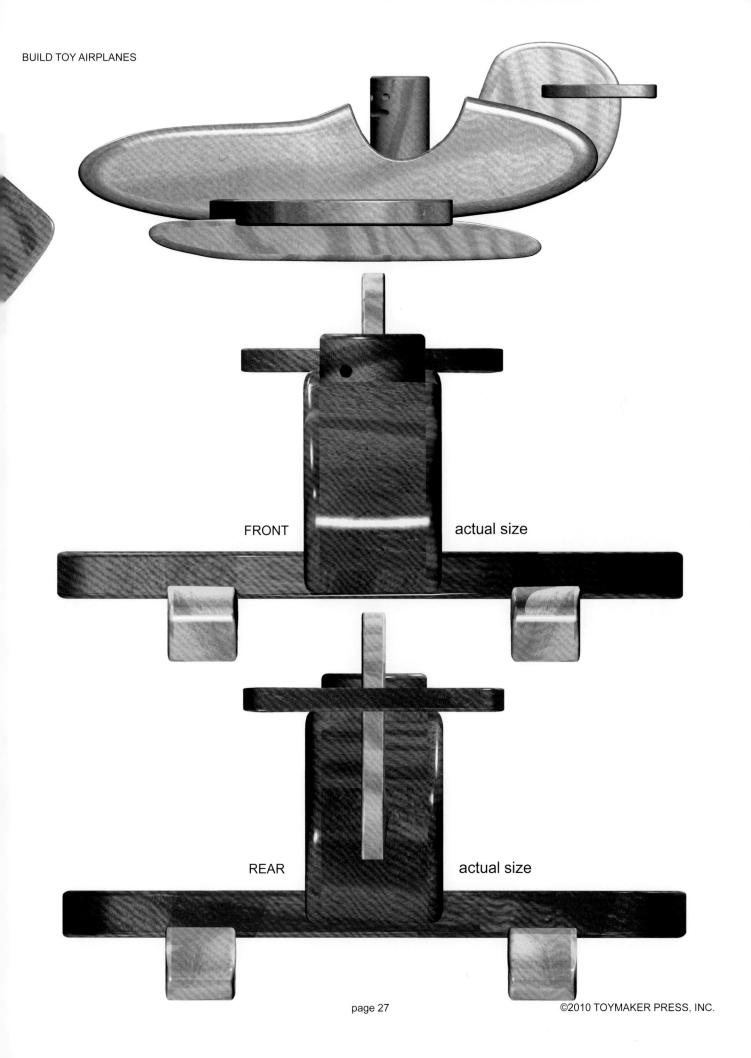

FRONT   actual size

REER   actual size

BUILD TOY AIRPLANES

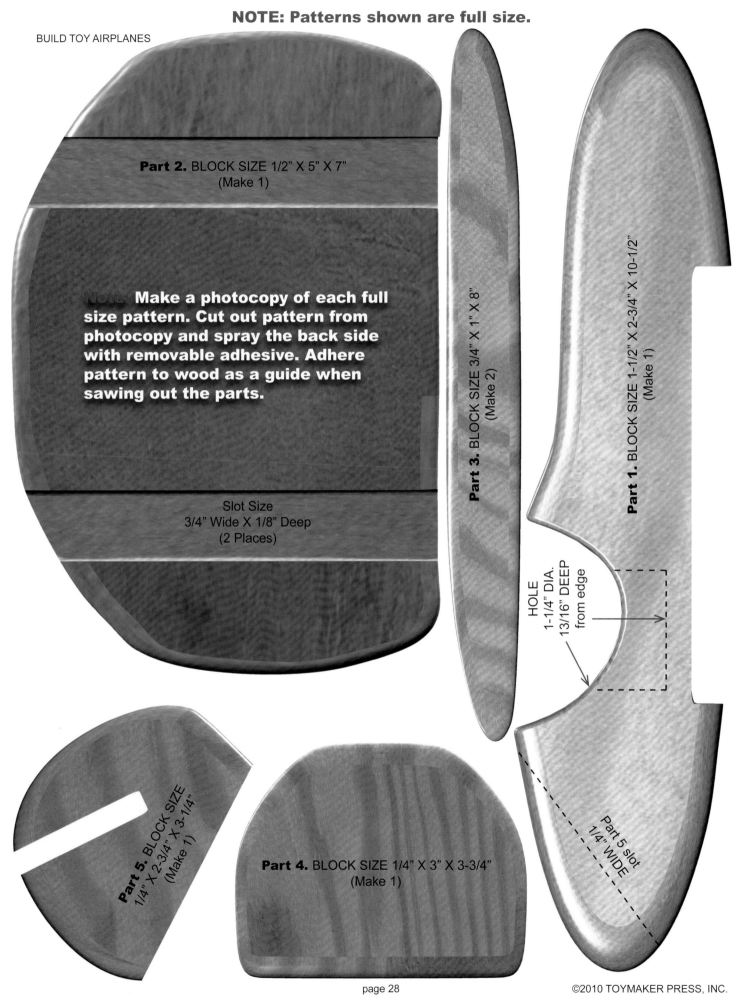

Part 2. BLOCK SIZE 1/2" X 5" X 7"
(Make 1)

Make a photocopy of each full size pattern. Cut out pattern from photocopy and spray the back side with removable adhesive. Adhere pattern to wood as a guide when sawing out the parts.

Slot Size
3/4" Wide X 1/8" Deep
(2 Places)

Part 3. BLOCK SIZE 3/4" X 1" X 8"
(Make 2)

Part 1. BLOCK SIZE 1-1/2" X 2-3/4" X 10-1/2"
(Make 1)

HOLE
1-1/4" DIA.
13/16" DEEP
from edge

Part 5 slot
1/4" WIDE

Part 5. BLOCK SIZE
1/4" X 2-3/4" X 3-1/4"
(Make 1)

Part 4. BLOCK SIZE 1/4" X 3" X 3-3/4"
(Make 1)

NOTE: All dimensions are for block size prior to cutting to shape.

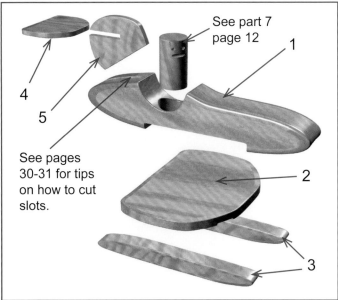

See part 7
page 12

4

5

See pages
30-31 for tips
on how to cut
slots.

1

2

3

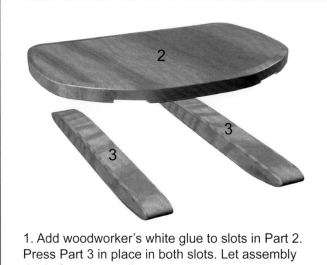

2

3

3

1. Add woodworker's white glue to slots in Part 2.
Press Part 3 in place in both slots. Let assembly
dry before proceeding.

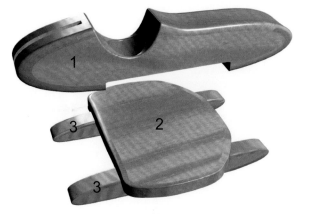

1

3

2

3

2. Apply woodworker's white glue to large slot in
bottom of Part 1. Press Part 1 into position in the
middle of the assembly as shown above. Let dry.

5

1

2

3

3. Apply woodworker's white glue to slot in top
rear of Part 1. Press Part 5 into position in the
slot in Part 1 as shown above. Let dry.

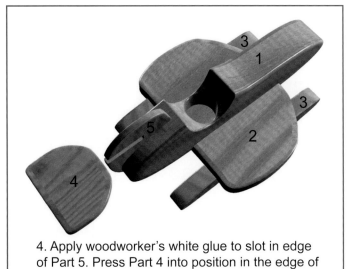

3

1

3

5

2

4

4. Apply woodworker's white glue to slot in edge
of Part 5. Press Part 4 into position in the edge of
Part 5 as shown above. Let dry.

TIPS & TECHNIQUES

Create accurate holes and slots in toy airplane parts by carefully following these steps.

For the best results use the best tools. Drill holes in toys using a saw tooth drill bit like the one shown above. There are numerous high quality hand and power tools available for drilling and sawing. Hard wearing professional quality drill bits and saw blades are the best choices for long production runs.

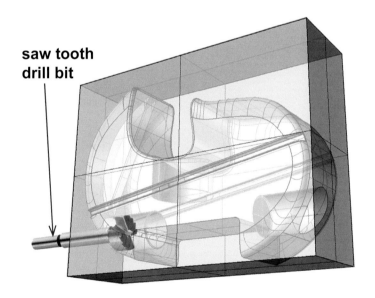

saw tooth drill bit

slot bottom

Saw off end of block at same angle as slot bottom.

Make a wood block that is larger than the toy pattern. Using the pattern photocopy as a guide, mark the position of holes with a pencil or marker. Drill holes to correct depth.

Create a mark on the block with a pencil or marker at the same angle as the bottom of the slot to be sawn. The block sawing angle is shown as a red broken line in the drawing.

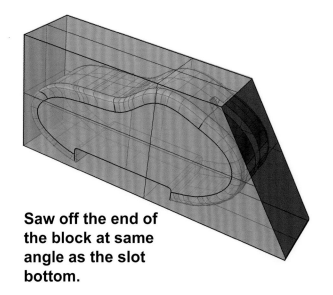

Saw off the end of the block at same angle as the slot bottom.

The sawn angle is a perfect base for aligning the saw blade at the correct angle and depth of cut. A table saw works best for this procedure.

A hand saw can also be used to cut slots by first clamping the block in a vise with the angle side up. Excess wood is removed with a small chisel.

Use a table saw, rip fence and multiple passes to cut an accurate tail slot in the fuselage.

A table saw blade and cross-cut guide make tight fitting wing slots.

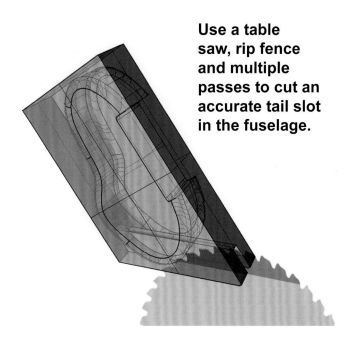

For narrow slots set the saw blade to correct height for depth of slot then slide the block along the rip fence while pressing the angled cut against the saw table top.

The wider slots can be sawn by using the cross-cut guide on the table saw combined with multiple passes through the blade to cut away the material to form the slot.

ZIPPER

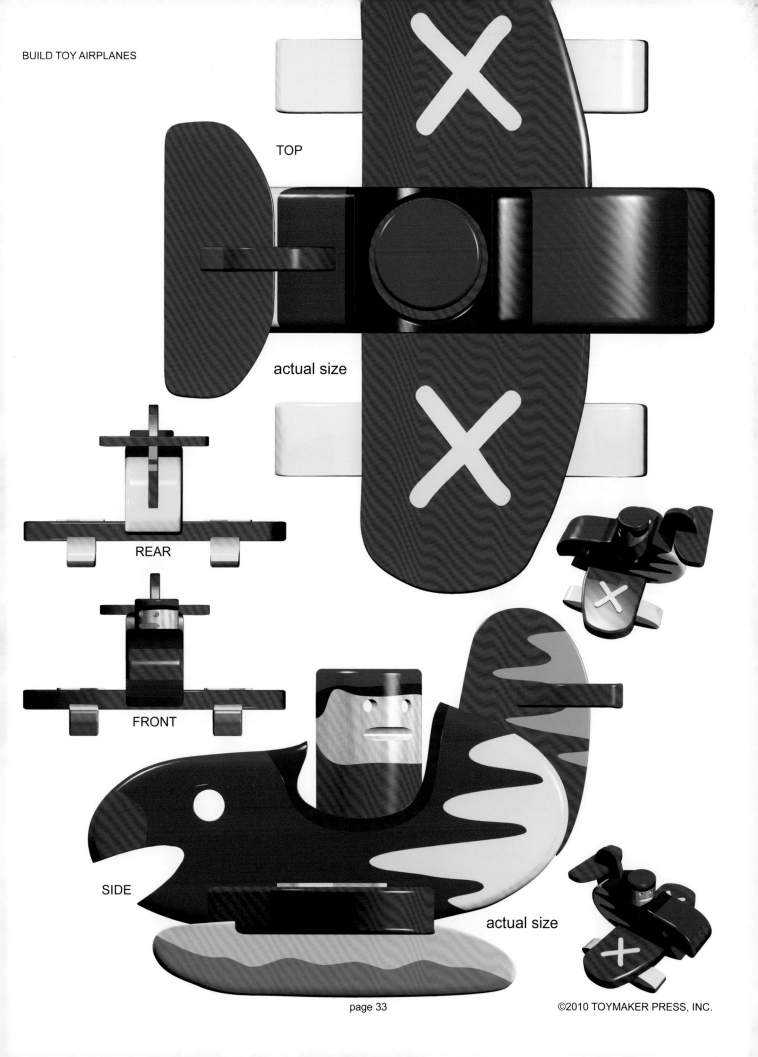

BUILD TOY AIRPLANES

TOP

actual size

REAR

FRONT

SIDE

actual size

NOTE: Patterns shown are full size.

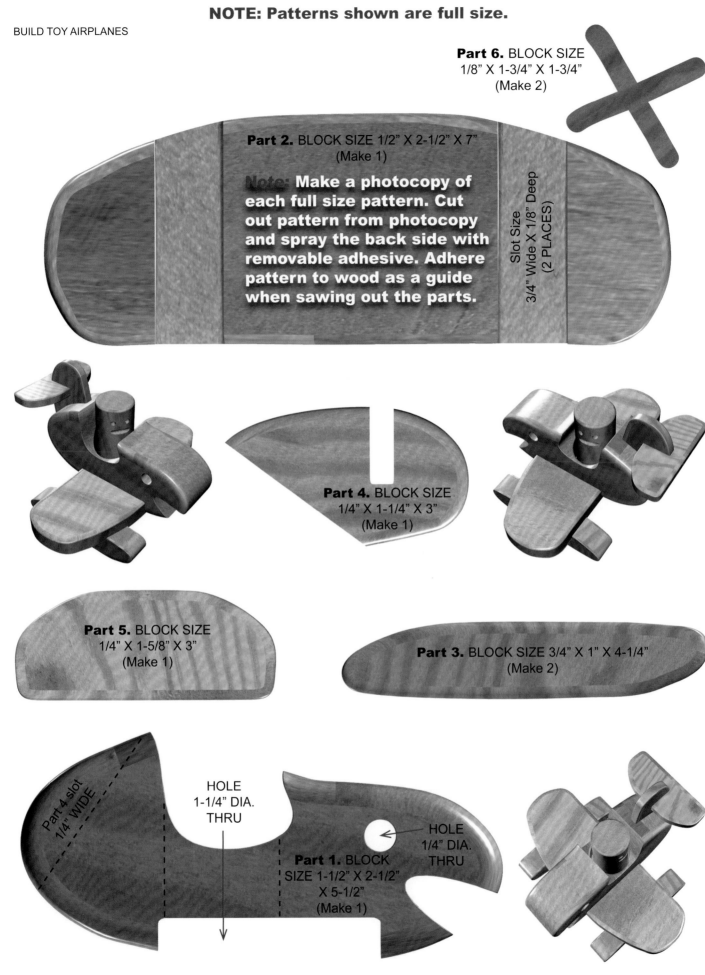

Part 6. BLOCK SIZE
1/8" X 1-3/4" X 1-3/4"
(Make 2)

Part 2. BLOCK SIZE 1/2" X 2-1/2" X 7"
(Make 1)

Note: Make a photocopy of each full size pattern. Cut out pattern from photocopy and spray the back side with removable adhesive. Adhere pattern to wood as a guide when sawing out the parts.

Slot Size
3/4" Wide X 1/8" Deep
(2 PLACES)

Part 4. BLOCK SIZE
1/4" X 1-1/4" X 3"
(Make 1)

Part 5. BLOCK SIZE
1/4" X 1-5/8" X 3"
(Make 1)

Part 3. BLOCK SIZE 3/4" X 1" X 4-1/4"
(Make 2)

Part 4 slot
1/4" WIDE

HOLE
1-1/4" DIA.
THRU

HOLE
1/4" DIA.
THRU

Part 1. BLOCK
SIZE 1-1/2" X 2-1/2"
X 5-1/2"
(Make 1)

NOTE: All dimensions are for block size prior to cutting to shape.

BUILD TOY AIRPLANES

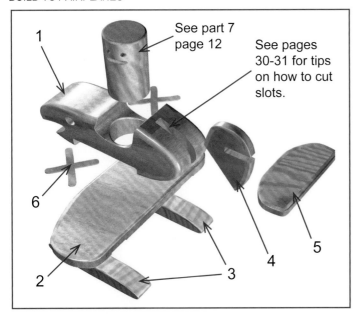

1

See part 7
page 12

See pages
30-31 for tips
on how to cut
slots.

6

2

3

4

5

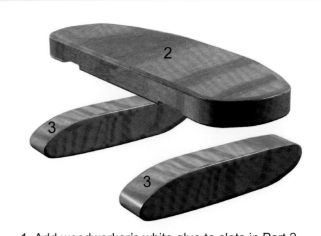

2

3

3

1. Add woodworker's white glue to slots in Part 2. Press Part 3 in place in both slots. Let assembly dry before proceeding.

1

2

3

3

2. Apply woodworker's white glue to large slot in bottom of Part 1. Press Part 1 into position in the middle of the assembly as shown above. Let dry.

4

1

2

3

3. Apply woodworker's white glue to slot in top of Part 1. Press Part 4 into position in the slot in Part 1 as shown above. Let dry.

4

5

1

2

3

4. Apply woodworker's white glue to tail slot in edge of Part 4. Press Part 5 into position in the slot in Part 4 as shown above. Let dry.

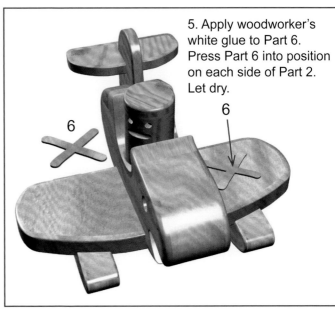

5. Apply woodworker's white glue to Part 6. Press Part 6 into position on each side of Part 2. Let dry.

6

6

SKY KING

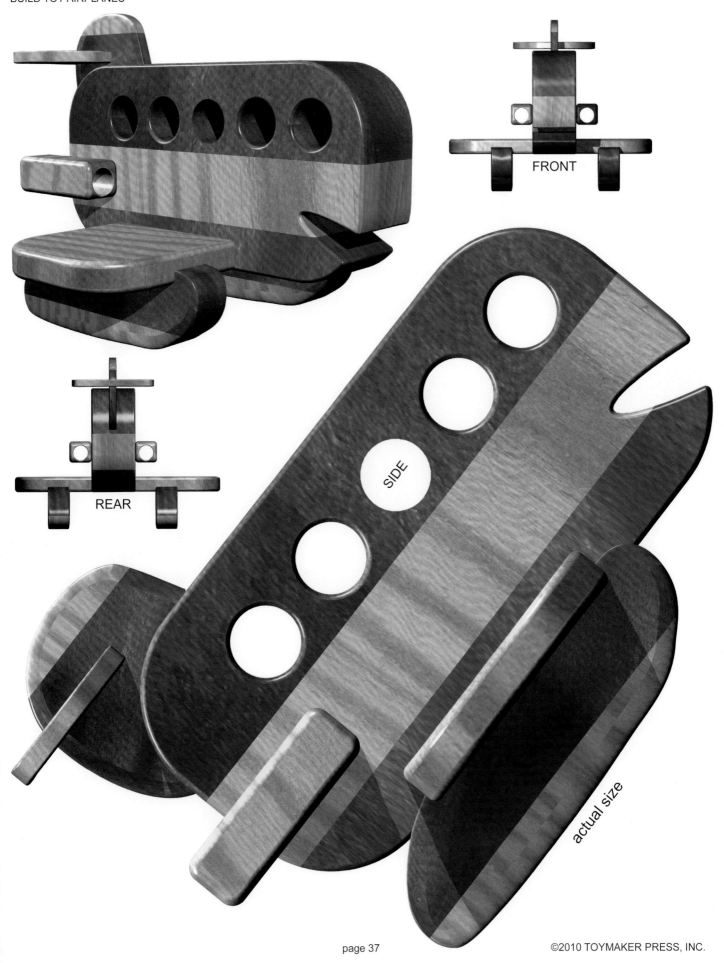

FRONT

REAR

SIDE

actual size

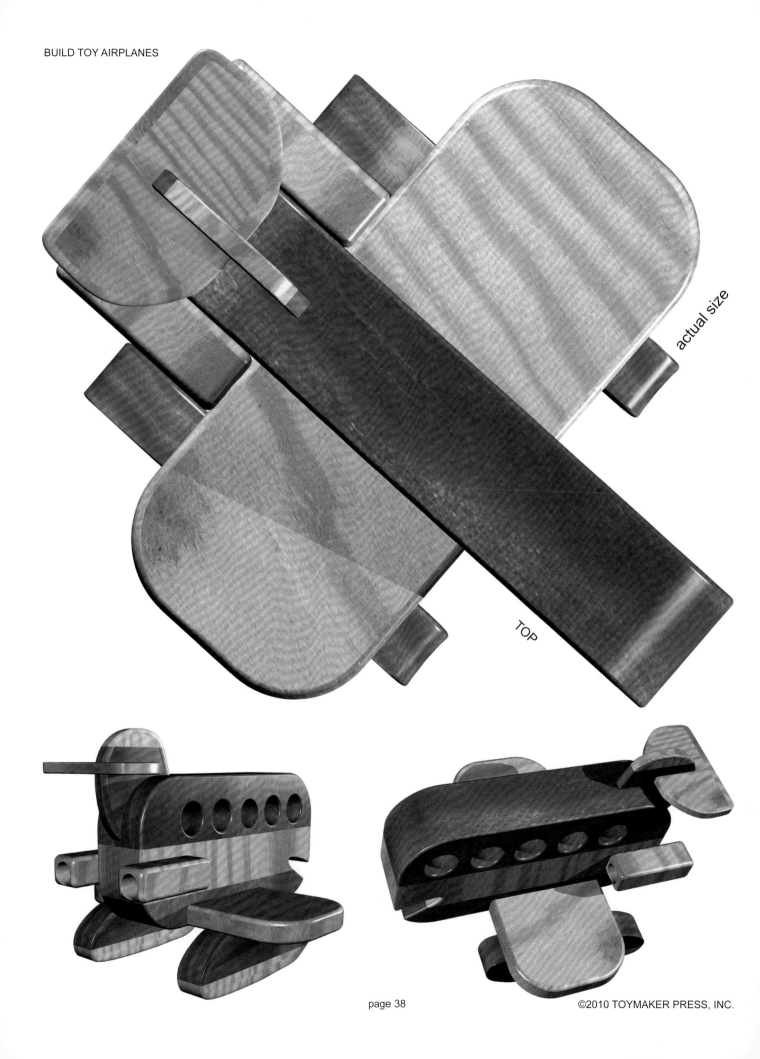

actual size

TOP

NOTE: Patterns shown are full size.

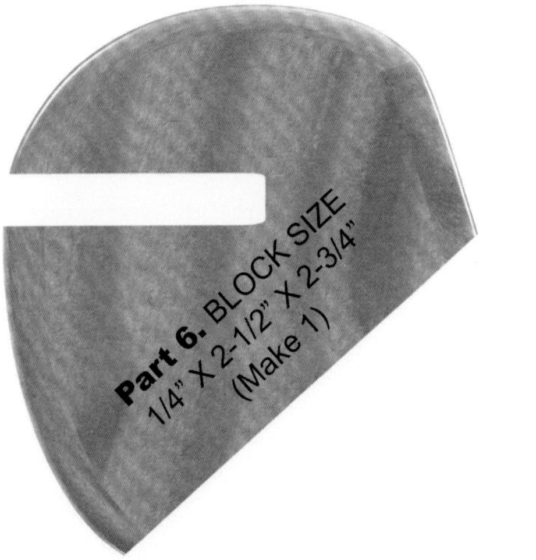

Part 6. BLOCK SIZE
1/4" X 2-1/2" X 2-3/4"
(Make 1)

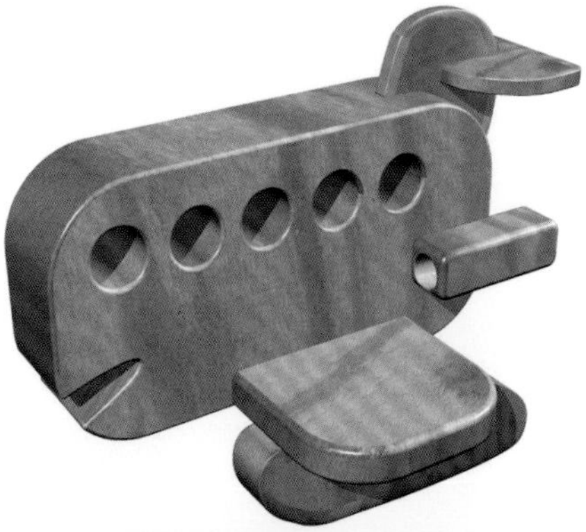

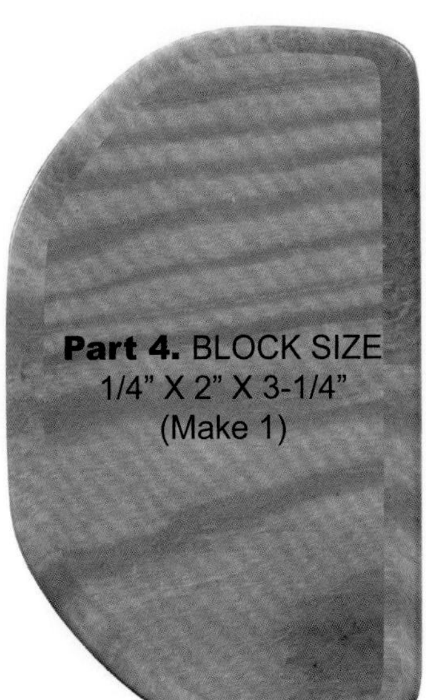

Part 4. BLOCK SIZE
1/4" X 2" X 3-1/4"
(Make 1)

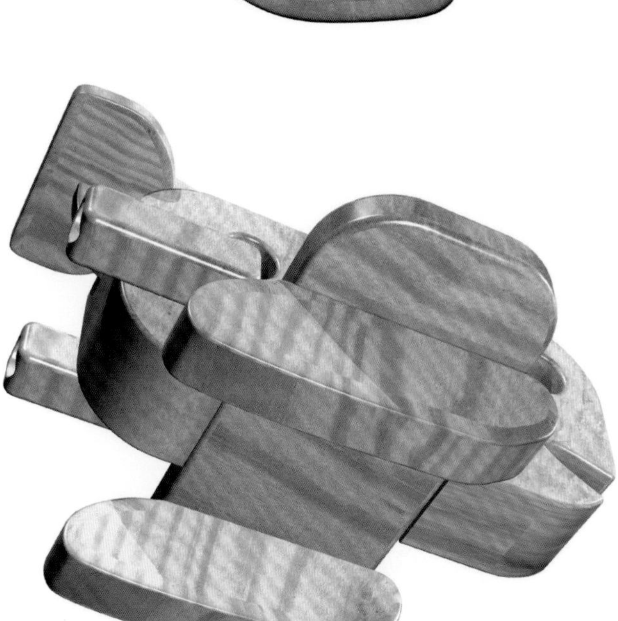

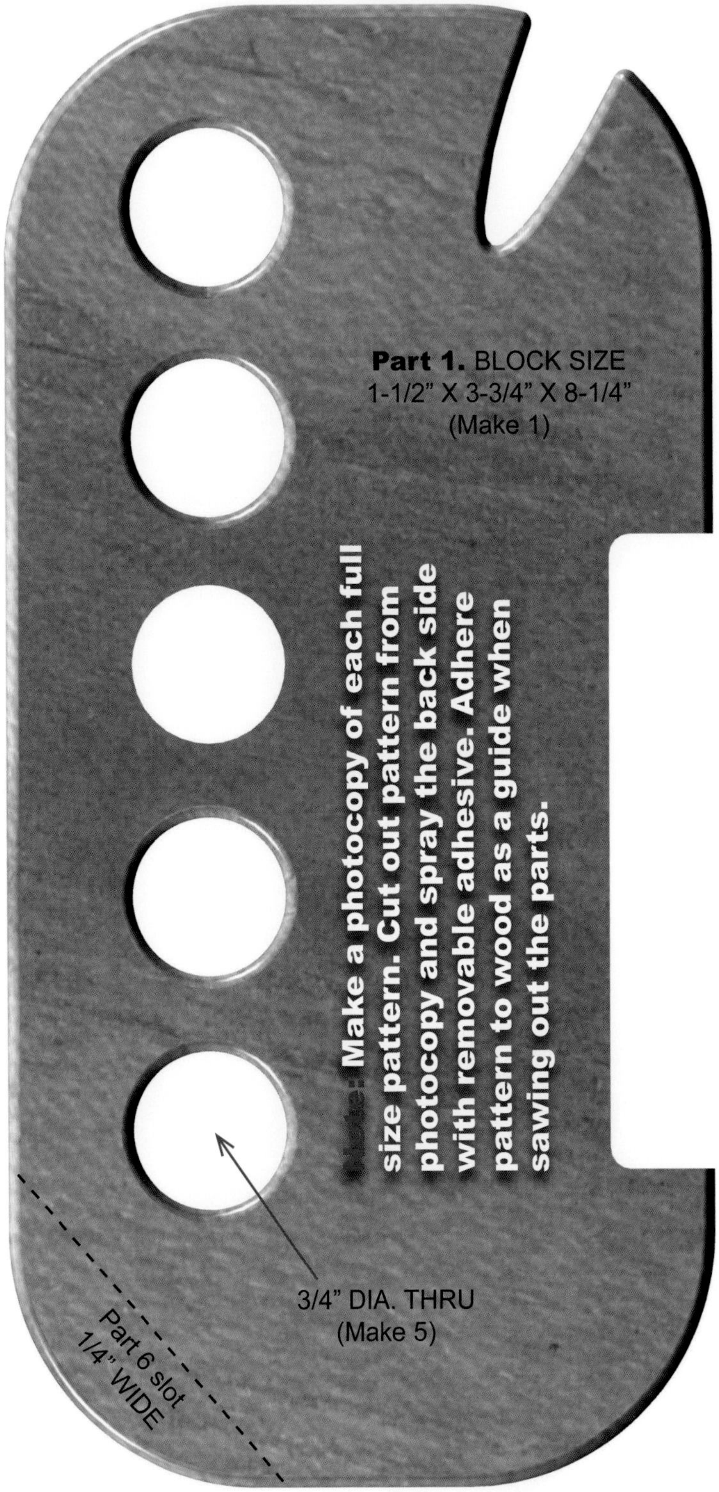

Part 1. BLOCK SIZE
1-1/2" X 3-3/4" X 8-1/4"
(Make 1)
Note: Make a photocopy of each full size pattern. Cut out pattern from photocopy and spray the back side with removable adhesive. Adhere pattern to wood as a guide when sawing out the parts.
3/4" DIA. THRU
(Make 5)
Part 6 slot
1/4" WIDE

NOTE: All dimensions are for block size prior to cutting to shape.

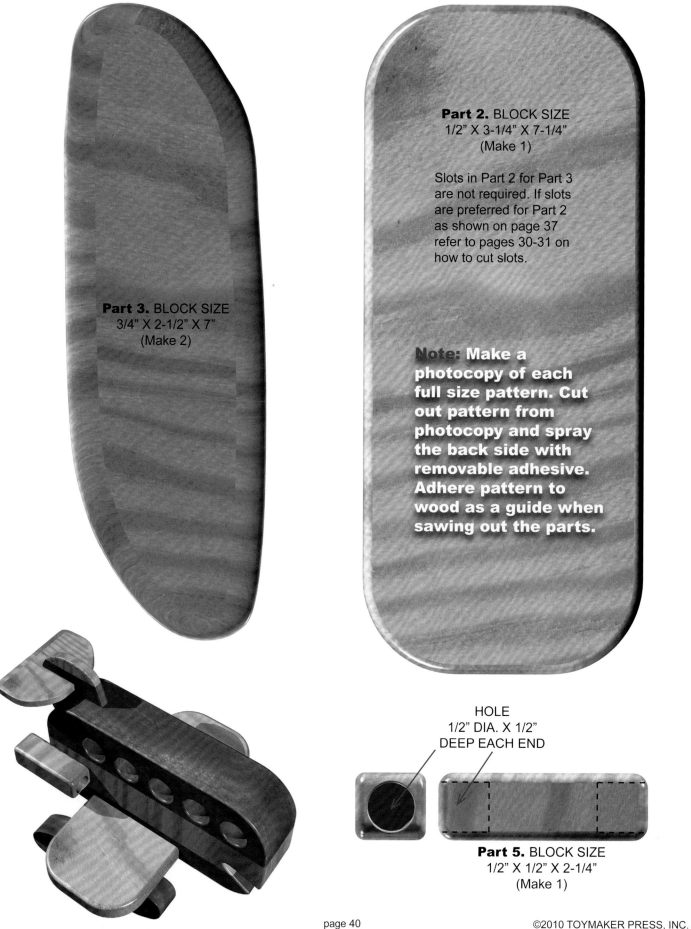

Part 3. BLOCK SIZE
3/4" X 2-1/2" X 7"
(Make 2)

Part 2. BLOCK SIZE
1/2" X 3-1/4" X 7-1/4"
(Make 1)

Slots in Part 2 for Part 3
are not required. If slots
are preferred for Part 2
as shown on page 37
refer to pages 30-31 on
how to cut slots.

Note: Make a
photocopy of each
full size pattern. Cut
out pattern from
photocopy and spray
the back side with
removable adhesive.
Adhere pattern to
wood as a guide when
sawing out the parts.

HOLE
1/2" DIA. X 1/2"
DEEP EACH END

Part 5. BLOCK SIZE
1/2" X 1/2" X 2-1/4"
(Make 1)

NOTE: All dimensions are for block size prior to cutting to shape.

BUILD TOY AIRPLANES

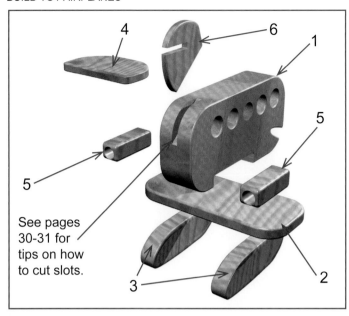

See pages 30-31 for tips on how to cut slots.

1. Add woodworker's white glue to the top of Part 3. Press Part 3 in place to bottom of Part 2 in two positions. Let assembly dry before proceeding.

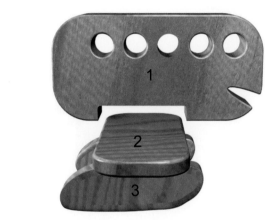

2. Apply woodworker's white glue to large slot in bottom of Part 1. Press Part 1 into position in the middle of the assembly as shown above. Let dry.

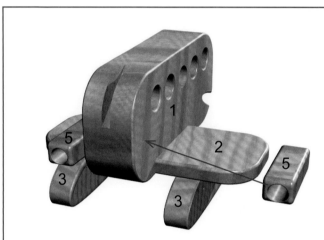

3. Apply woodworker's white glue to bottom of Part 5. Press Part 5 into position on each side of Part 1 as shown above. Let dry.

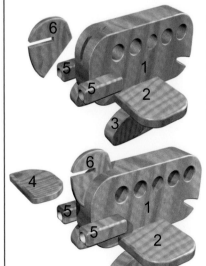

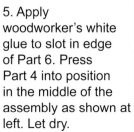

4. Apply woodworker's white glue to slot in edge of Part 1. Press Part 6 into position in the middle of Part 1 as shown at left. Let dry.

5. Apply woodworker's white glue to slot in edge of Part 6. Press Part 4 into position in the middle of the assembly as shown at left. Let dry.

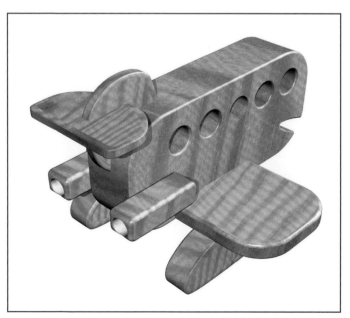

FREEDOM FIGHTER

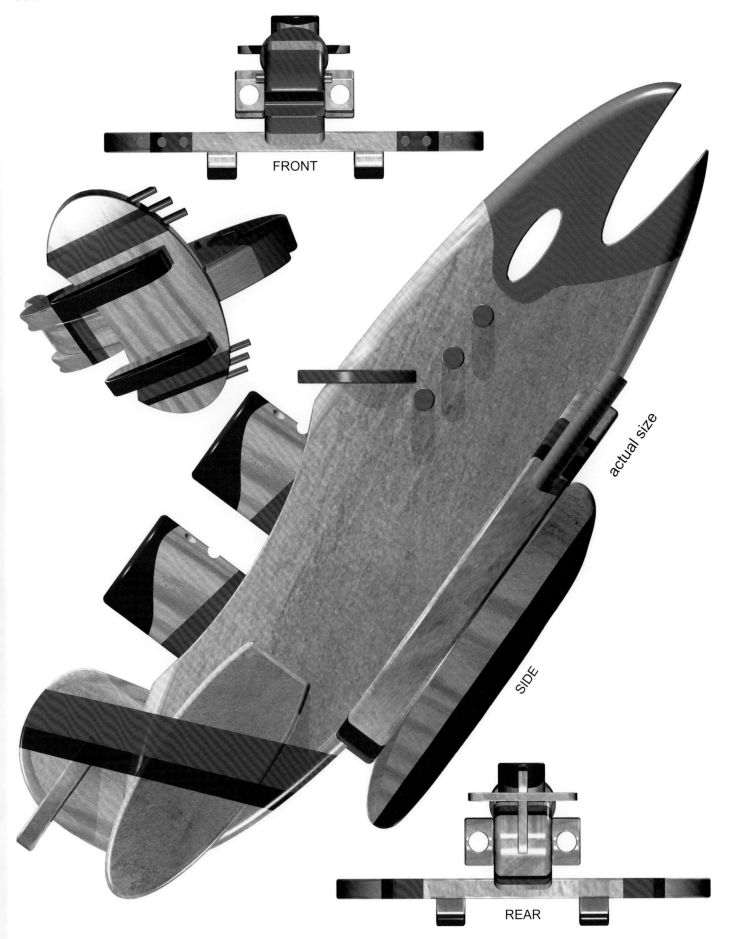

FRONT

actual size

SIDE

REAR

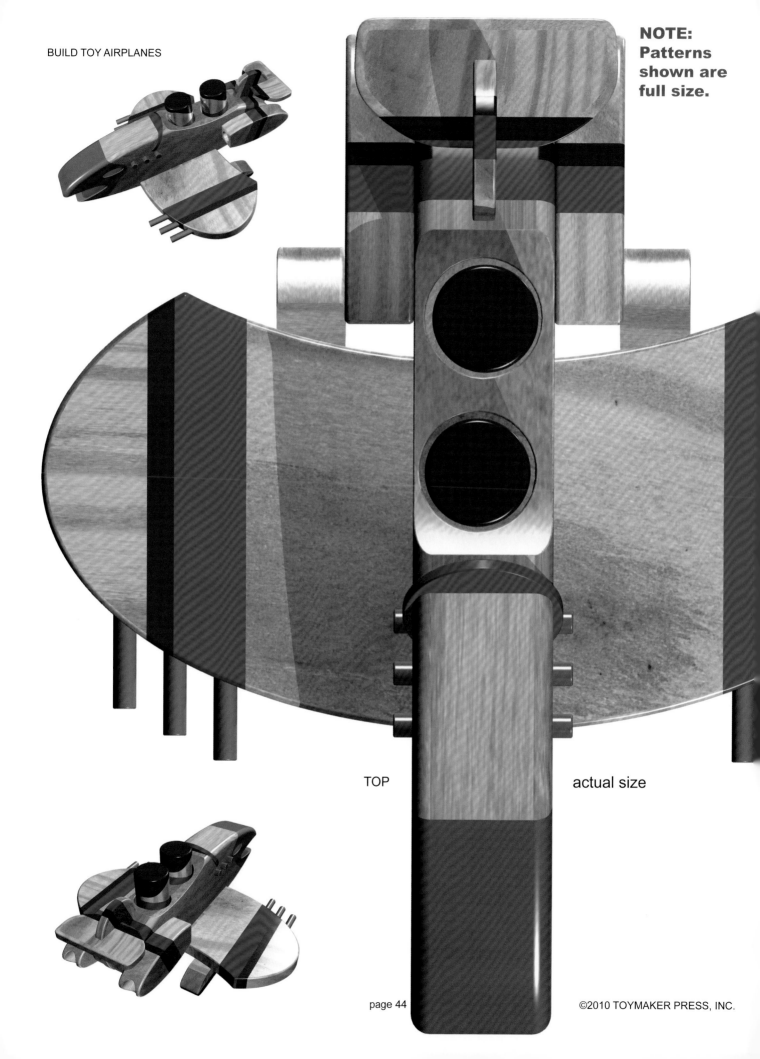

BUILD TOY AIRPLANES

TOP

actual size

NOTE: Patterns shown are full size.

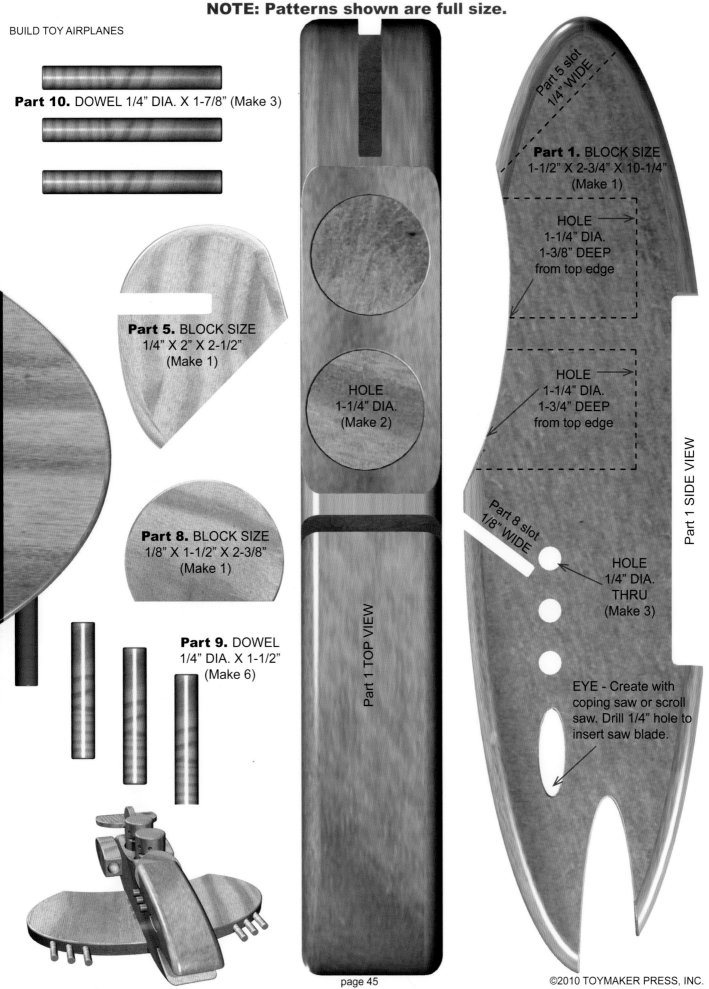

Part 10. DOWEL 1/4" DIA. X 1-7/8" (Make 3)

Part 5. BLOCK SIZE
1/4" X 2" X 2-1/2"
(Make 1)

Part 8. BLOCK SIZE
1/8" X 1-1/2" X 2-3/8"
(Make 1)

Part 9. DOWEL
1/4" DIA. X 1-1/2"
(Make 6)

HOLE
1-1/4" DIA.
(Make 2)

Part 1 TOP VIEW

Part 5 slot
1/4" WIDE

Part 1. BLOCK SIZE
1-1/2" X 2-3/4" X 10-1/4"
(Make 1)

HOLE
1-1/4" DIA.
1-3/8" DEEP
from top edge

HOLE
1-1/4" DIA.
1-3/4" DEEP
from top edge

Part 1 SIDE VIEW

Part 8 slot
1/8" WIDE

HOLE
1/4" DIA.
THRU
(Make 3)

EYE - Create with
coping saw or scroll
saw. Drill 1/4" hole to
insert saw blade.

NOTE: All dimensions are for block size prior to cutting to shape.

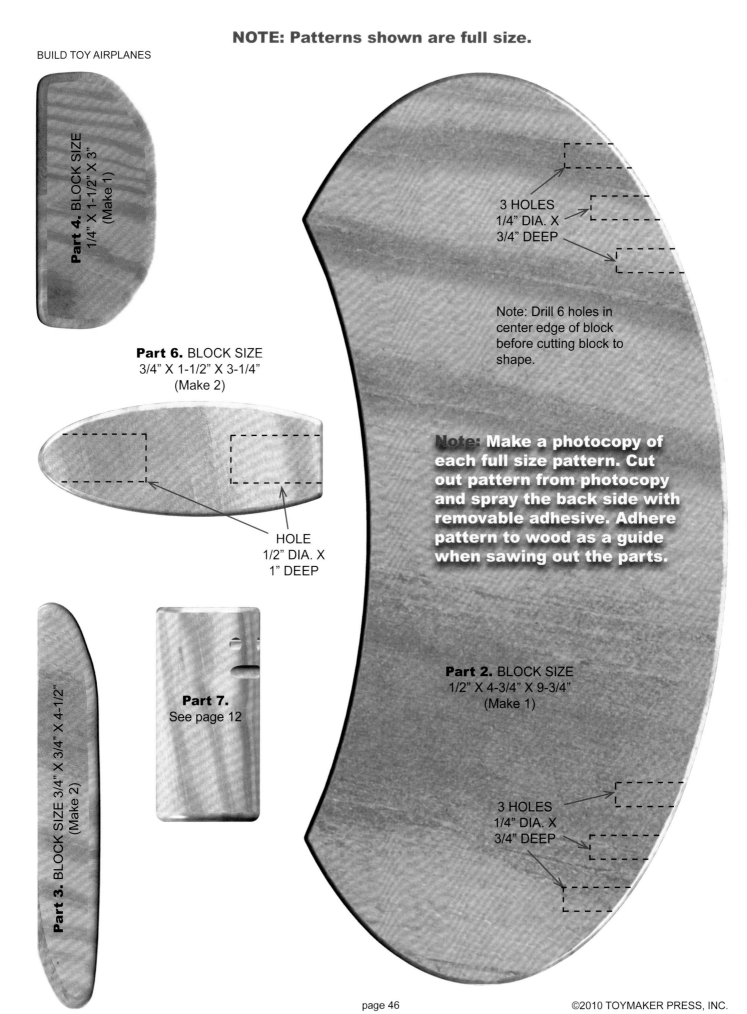

BUILD TOY AIRPLANES

Part 4. BLOCK SIZE
1/4" X 1-1/2" X 3"
(Make 1)

Part 6. BLOCK SIZE
3/4" X 1-1/2" X 3-1/4"
(Make 2)

HOLE
1/2" DIA. X
1" DEEP

Part 3. BLOCK SIZE 3/4" X 3/4" X 4-1/2"
(Make 2)

Part 7.
See page 12

3 HOLES
1/4" DIA. X
3/4" DEEP

Note: Drill 6 holes in
center edge of block
before cutting block to
shape.

Note: Make a photocopy of
each full size pattern. Cut
out pattern from photocopy
and spray the back side with
removable adhesive. Adhere
pattern to wood as a guide
when sawing out the parts.

Part 2. BLOCK SIZE
1/2" X 4-3/4" X 9-3/4"
(Make 1)

3 HOLES
1/4" DIA. X
3/4" DEEP

NOTE: All dimensions are for block size prior to cutting to shape.

BUILD TOY AIRPLANES

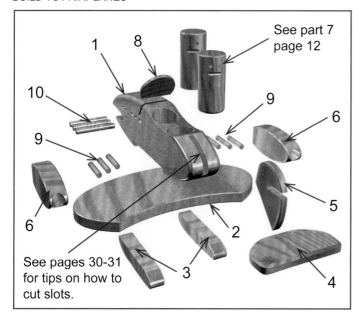

See part 7
page 12

See pages 30-31
for tips on how to
cut slots.

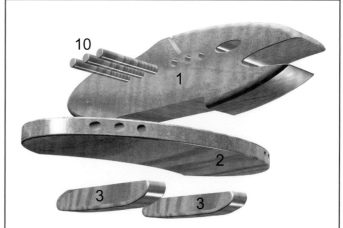

1. Add woodworker's white glue to top of Part 3. Press Part 3 in place in two positions on bottom of Part 2. Let dry before proceeding.

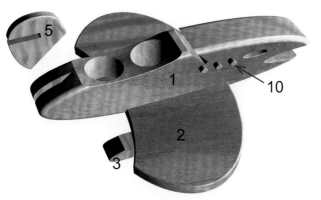

2. Apply woodworker's white glue to large slot in bottom of Part 1. Press Part 1 into position in the middle of the assembly shown above. Let dry. Apply glue to 3 holes in side of Part 1. Press Part 10 into position in 3 places in Part 1. Let dry.

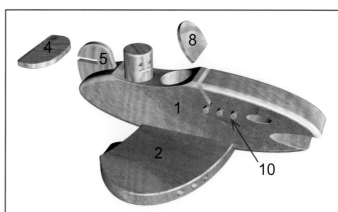

3. Apply woodworker's white glue to both slots in top of Part 1. Press Parts 5 & 8 into position in Part 1 as shown above. Let dry. Apply glue to slot in Part 5. Press Part 4 into position in Part 5. Let dry before proceeding.

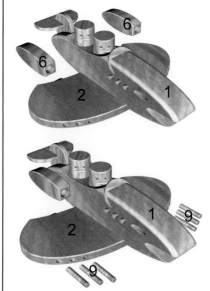

4. Apply woodworker's white glue to inside edges of Part 6. Press Part 6 into position on each side of Part 1 as shown at left. Let dry.

5. Apply a spot of woodworker's white glue to 6 holes in front edge of Part 2. Press Part 9 into 6 holes in edge of Part 2. Let dry.

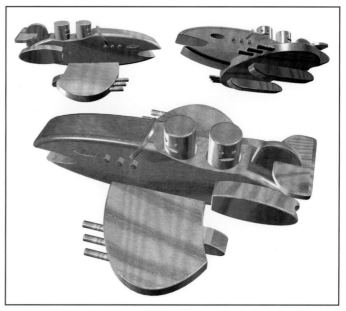

STUNT RIDER

BUILD TOY AIRPLANES

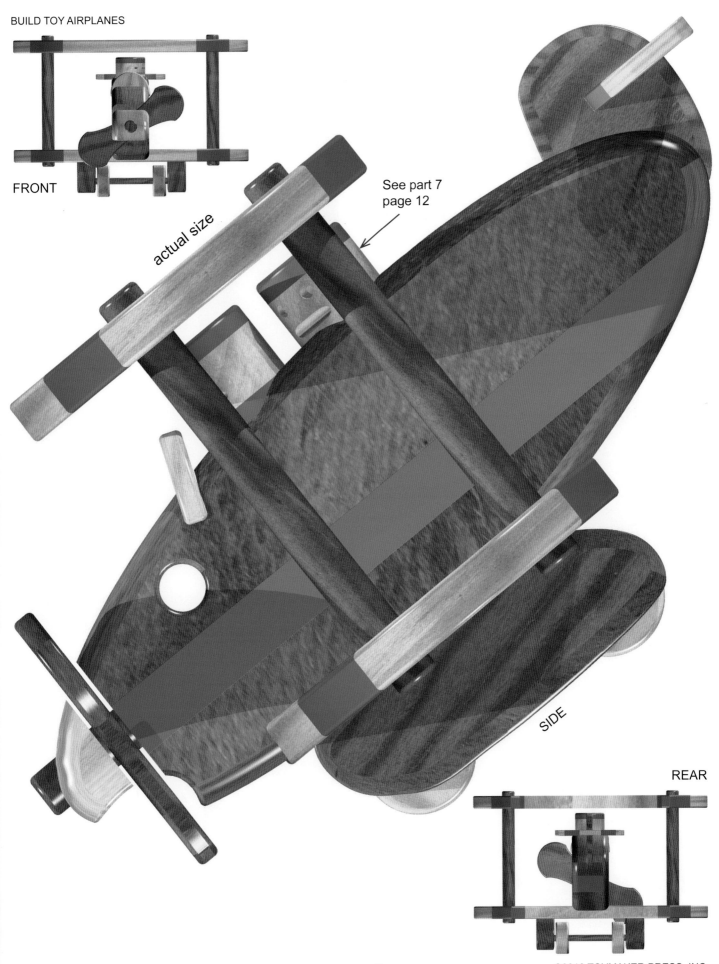

FRONT

actual size

See part 7
page 12

SIDE

REAR

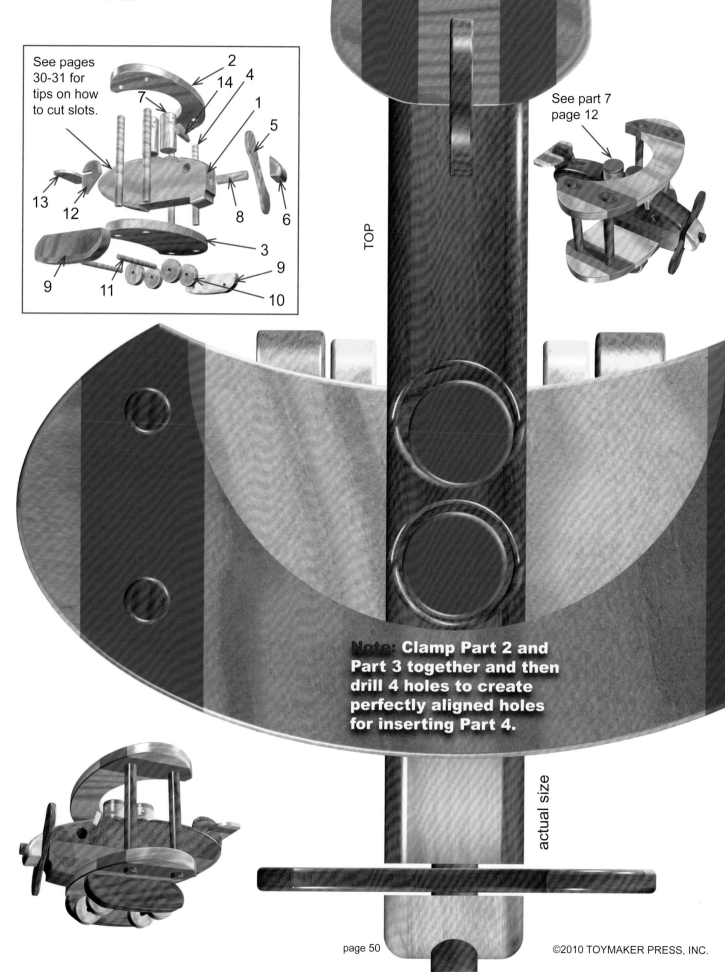

See pages 30-31 for tips on how to cut slots.

See part 7 page 12

TOP

Note: Clamp Part 2 and Part 3 together and then drill 4 holes to create perfectly aligned holes for inserting Part 4.

actual size

NOTE: Patterns shown are full size.

BUILD TOY AIRPLANES

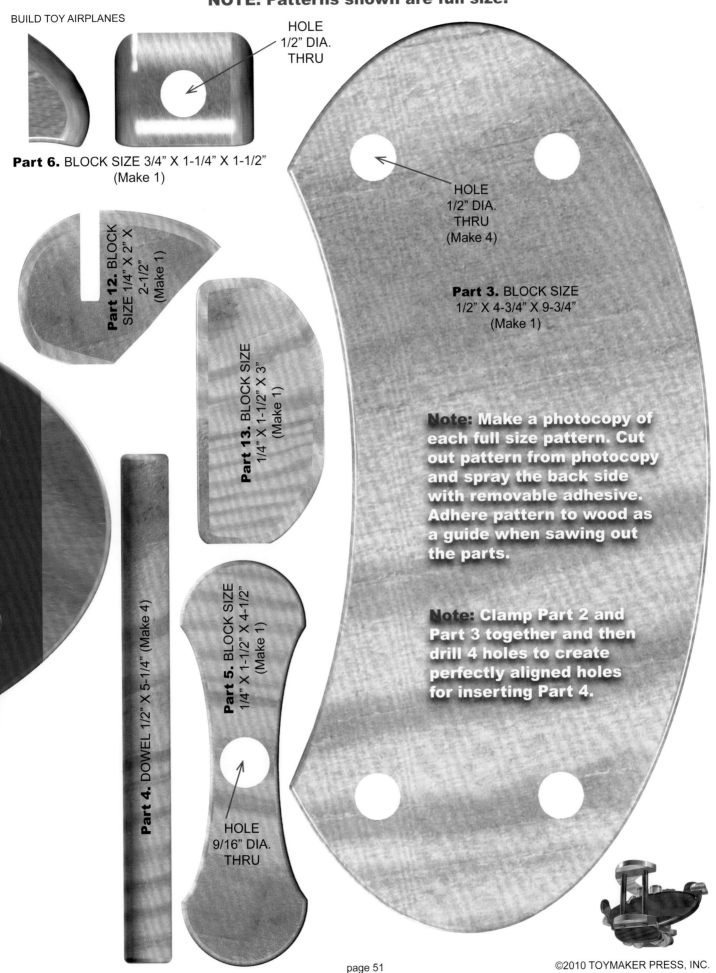

HOLE
1/2" DIA.
THRU

Part 6. BLOCK SIZE 3/4" X 1-1/4" X 1-1/2"
(Make 1)

HOLE
1/2" DIA.
THRU
(Make 4)

Part 3. BLOCK SIZE
1/2" X 4-3/4" X 9-3/4"
(Make 1)

Part 12. BLOCK SIZE 1/4" X 2" X 2-1/2" (Make 1)

Part 13. BLOCK SIZE 1/4" X 1-1/2" X 3" (Make 1)

Part 4. DOWEL 1/2" X 5-1/4" (Make 4)

Part 5. BLOCK SIZE 1/4" X 1-1/2" X 4-1/2" (Make 1)

HOLE
9/16" DIA.
THRU

Note: Make a photocopy of each full size pattern. Cut out pattern from photocopy and spray the back side with removable adhesive. Adhere pattern to wood as a guide when sawing out the parts.

Note: Clamp Part 2 and Part 3 together and then drill 4 holes to create perfectly aligned holes for inserting Part 4.

NOTE: All dimensions are for block size prior to cutting to shape.

BUILD TOY AIRPLANES

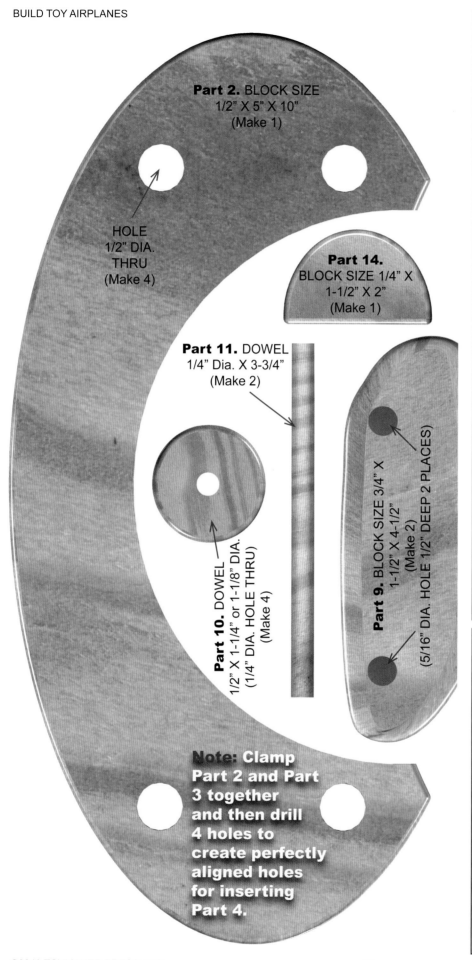

Part 2. BLOCK SIZE
1/2" X 5" X 10"
(Make 1)

HOLE
1/2" DIA.
THRU
(Make 4)

Part 14.
BLOCK SIZE 1/4" X
1-1/2" X 2"
(Make 1)

Part 11. DOWEL
1/4" Dia. X 3-3/4"
(Make 2)

Part 10. DOWEL
1/2" X 1-1/4" or 1-1/8" DIA.
(1/4" DIA. HOLE THRU)
(Make 4)

Part 9. BLOCK SIZE 3/4" X
1-1/2" X 4-1/2"
(Make 2)
(5/16" DIA. HOLE 1/2" DEEP 2 PLACES)

**Note: Clamp
Part 2 and Part
3 together
and then drill
4 holes to
create perfectly
aligned holes
for inserting
Part 4.**

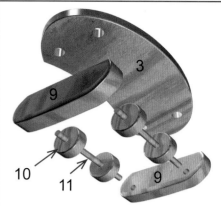

1. Glue 4 wheels solidly to axles as shown. Axles rotate freely in Part 9. Add glue to tops of Part 9 and press each Part 9 in place on bottom of Part 3 with axles. Let assembly dry before proceeding.

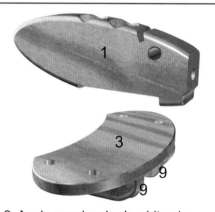

2. Apply woodworker's white glue to large slot in bottom of Part 1. Press Part 1 into position on Part 3 in the middle of the assembly shown above. Let dry.

3. Apply woodworker's white glue to slots in top of Part 1. Press Part 12 into position in Part 1 as shown in the assembly above. Let dry. Press Part 13 into slot in Part 12. Let dry. Press Part 14 into slot in Part 1. Let dry.

NOTE: All dimensions are for block size prior to cutting to shape.

BUILD TOY AIRPLANES

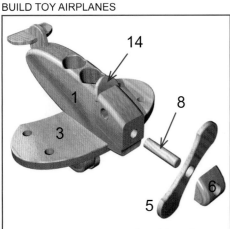

4. Apply woodworker's white glue to hole in front of Part 1. Press Part 8 into position into hole. Slide Part 5 over Part 8. Part 5 rotates freely. Add glue to end of Part 6. Press Part 6 onto Part 8. Let dry.

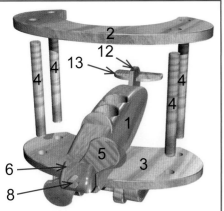

5. Apply woodworker's white glue to each end of each Part 4. Press each Part 4 into position in holes in Part 3. Press Part 2 over each Part 4. Let dry.

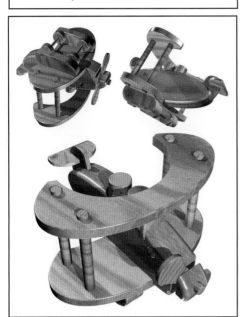

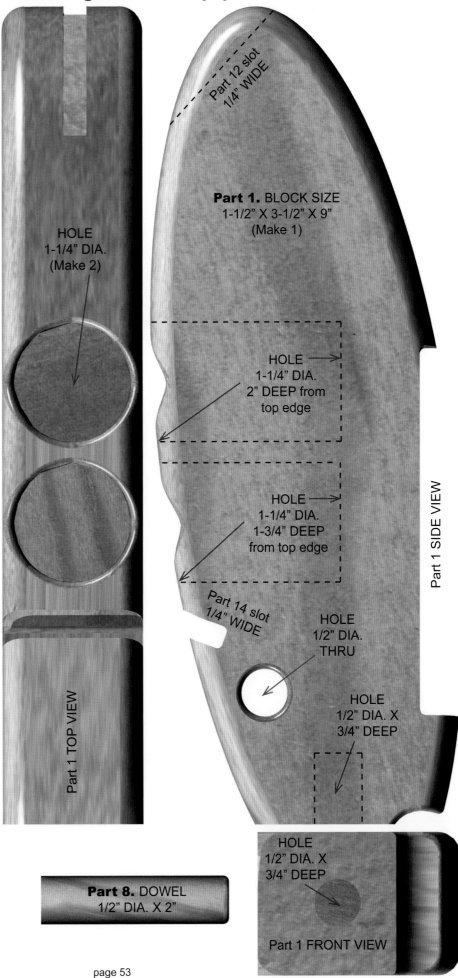

HOLE
1-1/4" DIA.
(Make 2)

Part 1 TOP VIEW

Part 12 slot
1/4" WIDE

Part 1. BLOCK SIZE
1-1/2" X 3-1/2" X 9"
(Make 1)

HOLE
1-1/4" DIA.
2" DEEP from
top edge

HOLE
1-1/4" DIA.
1-3/4" DEEP
from top edge

Part 14 slot
1/4" WIDE

HOLE
1/2" DIA.
THRU

HOLE
1/2" DIA. X
3/4" DEEP

Part 1 SIDE VIEW

HOLE
1/2" DIA. X
3/4" DEEP

Part 1 FRONT VIEW

Part 8. DOWEL
1/2" DIA. X 2"

NOTE: All dimensions are for block size prior to cutting to shape.

SPORT TWIN

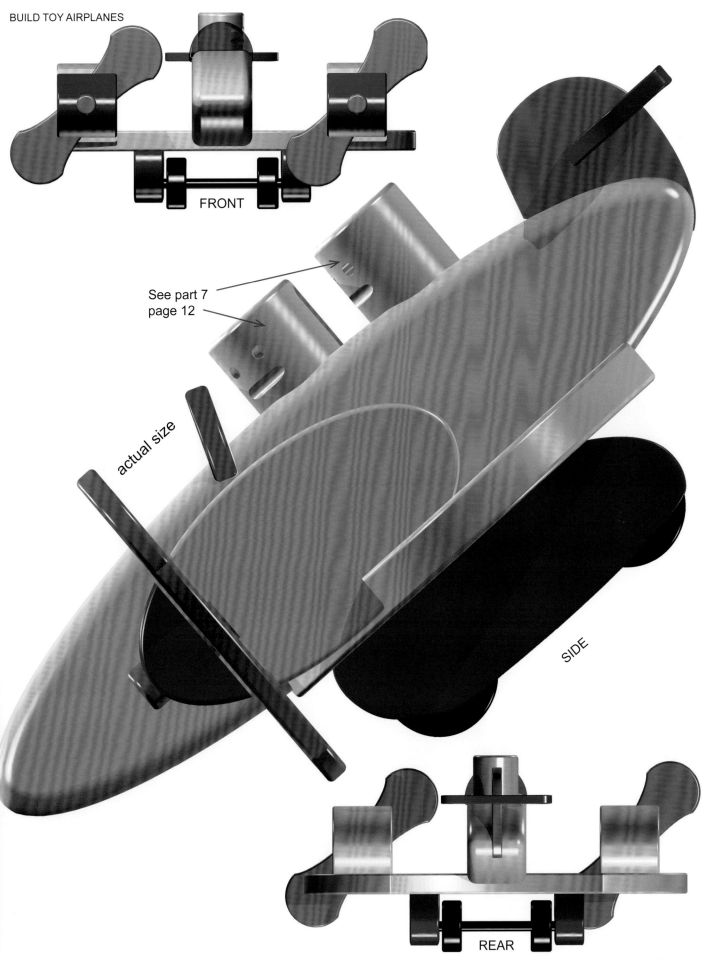

BUILD TOY AIRPLANES

FRONT

See part 7
page 12

actual size

SIDE

REAR

©2010 TOYMAKER PRESS, INC.

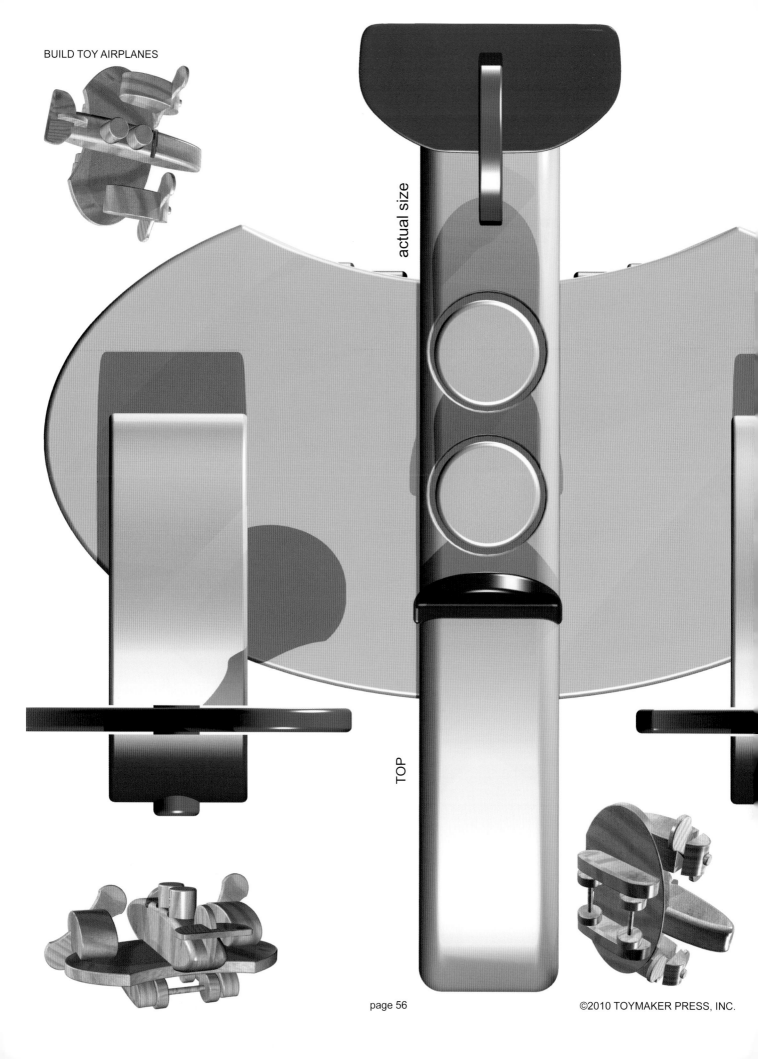

BUILD TOY AIRPLANES

actual size

TOP

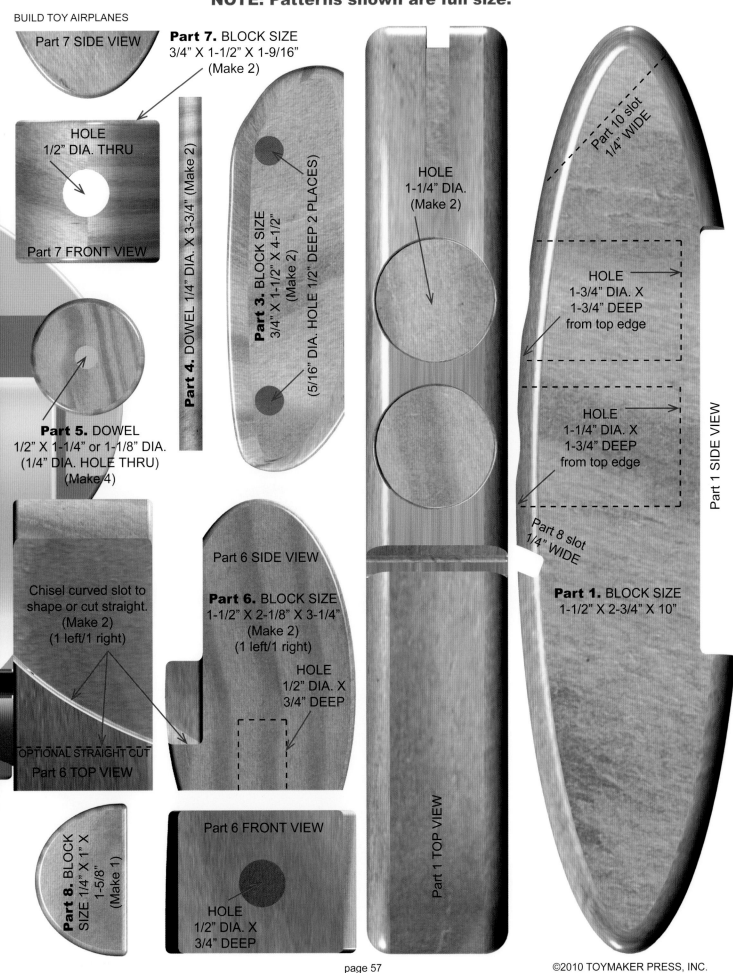

NOTE: Patterns shown are full size.

BUILD TOY AIRPLANES

Part 7 SIDE VIEW

Part 7. BLOCK SIZE
3/4" X 1-1/2" X 1-9/16"
(Make 2)

HOLE
1/2" DIA. THRU

Part 7 FRONT VIEW

Part 4. DOWEL 1/4" DIA. X 3-3/4" (Make 2)

Part 3. BLOCK SIZE
3/4" X 1-1/2" X 4-1/2"
(Make 2)
(5/16" DIA. HOLE 1/2" DEEP 2 PLACES)

HOLE
1-1/4" DIA.
(Make 2)

Part 10 slot
1/4" WIDE

HOLE
1-3/4" DIA. X
1-3/4" DEEP
from top edge

HOLE
1-1/4" DIA. X
1-3/4" DEEP
from top edge

Part 1 SIDE VIEW

Part 5. DOWEL
1/2" X 1-1/4" or 1-1/8" DIA.
(1/4" DIA. HOLE THRU)
(Make 4)

Chisel curved slot to
shape or cut straight.
(Make 2)
(1 left/1 right)

Part 6 SIDE VIEW

Part 6. BLOCK SIZE
1-1/2" X 2-1/8" X 3-1/4"
(Make 2)
(1 left/1 right)

HOLE
1/2" DIA. X
3/4" DEEP

Part 8 slot
1/4" WIDE

Part 1. BLOCK SIZE
1-1/2" X 2-3/4" X 10"

OPTIONAL STRAIGHT CUT
Part 6 TOP VIEW

Part 8. BLOCK
SIZE 1/4" X 1" X
1-5/8" (Make 1)

Part 6 FRONT VIEW

HOLE
1/2" DIA. X
3/4" DEEP

Part 1 TOP VIEW

©2010 TOYMAKER PRESS, INC.

NOTE: All dimensions are for block size prior to cutting to shape.

BUILD TOY AIRPLANES

Part 10. BLOCK SIZE 1/4" X 2" X 2-1/2" (Make 1)

Part 11. BLOCK SIZE 1/4" X 1-1/2" X 4-1/2" (Make 2)

HOLE 9/16" DIA. THRU

Part 12. DOWEL 1/2" DIA. X 2" (Make 2)

Part 2. BLOCK SIZE 1/2" X 5-1/4" X 9-3/4" (Make 1)

Note: Make a photocopy of each full size pattern. Cut out pattern from photocopy and spray the back side with removable adhesive. Adhere pattern to wood as a guide when sawing out the parts.

Part 9. BLOCK SIZE 1/4" X 1-1/2" X 3-1/4" (Make 1)

NOTE: All dimensions are for block size prior to cutting to shape.

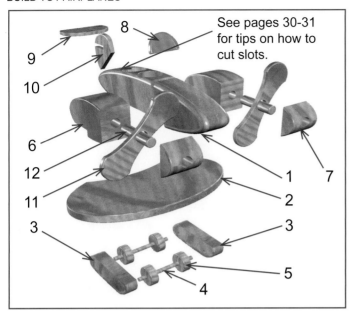

9
8
10
See pages 30-31 for tips on how to cut slots.
6
12
11
1
2
7
3
3
4
5

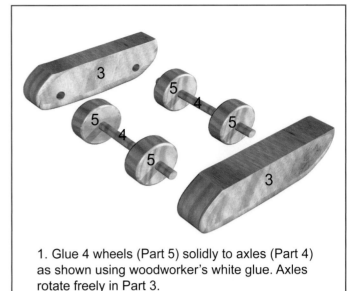

3
5
5
4
5
4
5
3

1. Glue 4 wheels (Part 5) solidly to axles (Part 4) as shown using woodworker's white glue. Axles rotate freely in Part 3.

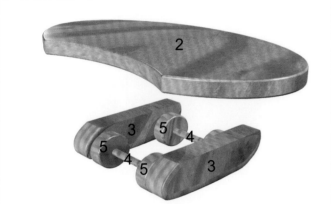

2
3
5
4
5
4
5
3

2. Add woodworker's white glue to tops of Part 3. Press Part 3 in place on bottom of Part 2 with axles turning smoothly. Let dry before proceeding.

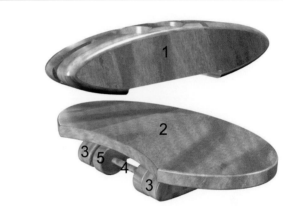

1
2
3
5
4
3

3. Apply woodworker's white glue to wide slot in bottom of Part 1. Press Part 1 into position in the middle of the assembly as shown above. Let dry.

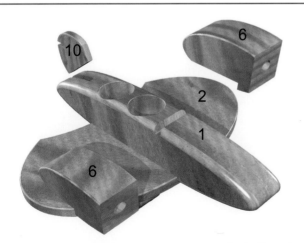

10
6
2
1
6

4. Apply woodworker's white glue to rear slot in Part 1. Insert Part 10 into rear slot in Part 1. Let dry. Apply glue to bottoms of Part 6. Press Part 6 into position on Part 2. Refer to Step 5: Apply glue to slot in Part 10. Insert Part 9 into Part 10. Insert Part 8 into slot in top of Part 1. Let dry.

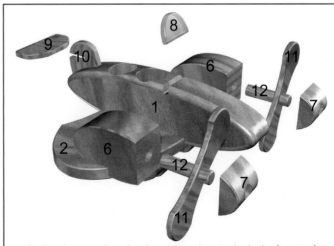

8
9
10
6
11
12
1
7
2
6
12
7
11

5. Apply woodworker's white glue to hole in front of each Part 6. Press Part 12 into position into each hole. Slide Part 11 over Part 12. Propellers rotate freely on shaft. Add glue to end of Part 12. Press Part 7 onto Part 12. Let dry.

NOTE: All dimensions are for block size prior to cutting to shape.

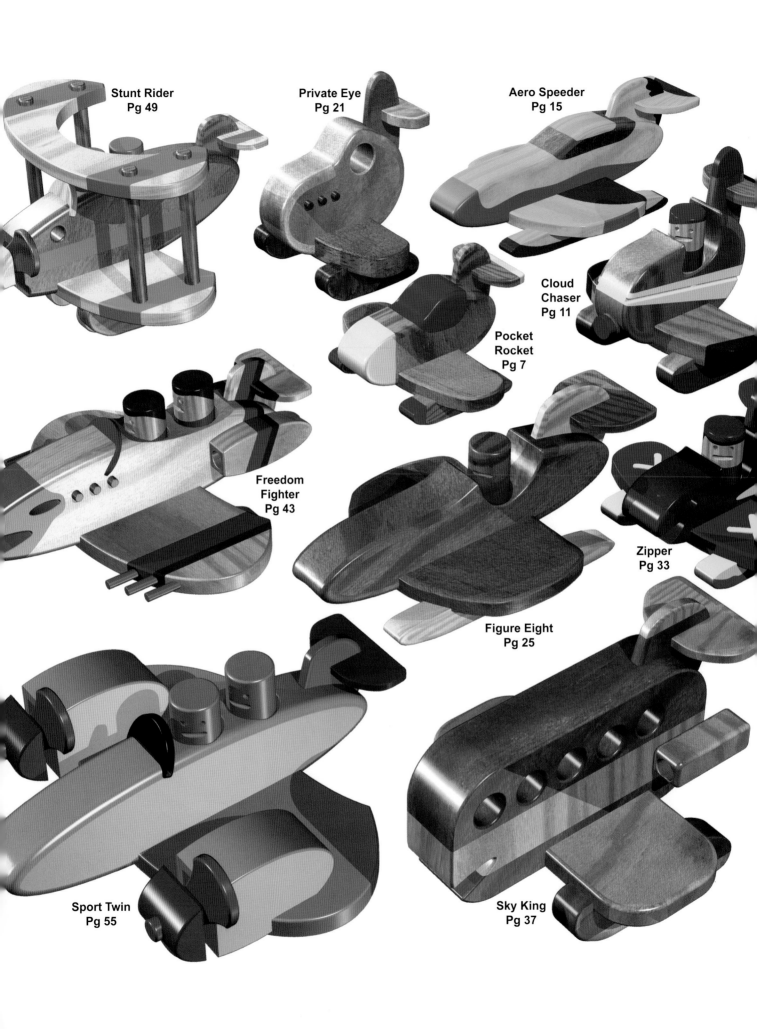

Stunt Rider
Pg 49

Private Eye
Pg 21

Aero Speeder
Pg 15

Cloud Chaser
Pg 11

Pocket Rocket
Pg 7

Freedom Fighter
Pg 43

Zipper
Pg 33

Figure Eight
Pg 25

Sport Twin
Pg 55

Sky King
Pg 37